Photo Finish

Photo Finish

*An Adventure in Biography
in Three Acts*

PETER USTINOV

LITTLE, BROWN AND COMPANY • BOSTON • TORONTO

Photographs by courtesy of Friedman-Abeles

Published simultaneously in Canada
by Little, Brown & Company (Canada) Limited

PRINTED IN THE UNITED STATES OF AMERICA

Photo Finish was first presented in New York City by Joseph E. Levine and Alfred de Liagre, Jr. at the Brooks Atkinson Theatre on the evening of February 12, 1963, with the following cast:

(*In Order of Appearance*)

STELLA	Eileen Herlie
SAM	Peter Ustinov
SAM ELDERLY	Dennis King
SAM MIDDLE-AGED	Donald Davis
SAM YOUNG	John Horton
CLARICE DONOHUE	Jessica Walter
ADA COONEY	Jessica Walter
REGINALD KINSALE, ESQ.	Paul Rogers
MRS. AGNES KINSALE	Cynthia Latham
TOMMY	John Horton
ALICE MONTEGO	Paddy Edwards

The action of the play, which is in three acts, takes place in the study of Kinsale House in London.

Act One

ACT ONE

A room in shadow. Illuminated is a bed, in which an OLD
MAN *is propped up with pillows. A wheelchair stands in
readiness near the bed, also a stick. An occasional table covered in medicine bottles, shining green, yellow, orange, red,
brown, as the reading lamp throws its light over and through
them. Left, illuminated by a desk lamp, is an imposing writing desk, covered with papers and a few books, and a telephone.*

As the action begins, the OLD MAN, *by name* SAM, *is staring at the audience with a long-suffering look while an*
ELDERLY LADY, *determined yet absent in manner, travels
hither and thither at a surprising pace. She is called* STELLA.
*The contrast between her energy and his lassitude is strik-
ing.*

STELLA
(Coming from bay window)

Now . . . no . . . yes . . . (*Pause*) On second thoughts no,
you won't need them . . . and yet, who knows, better be on
the safe side . . . (*She is at the bedside table*) . . . oh, you've
still got some . . . why didn't you tell me? All right, all right,
don't answer if you don't want to. . . . I'll tell you one thing,
though, young man, you don't take enough of them. They're
special ones and you know it. Dr. Beasley says they don't affect
the digestion or the heart . . . not that I usually trust him, still

3

I don't expect a doctor can go far wrong with aspirin . . . they're part of the cure of any arthritic condition. It says on the bottle they're made in Bristol, but actually they're Swiss. Drink your milk. (*Looking at the books on the floor*) Books. I don't know what you see in them . . . I can understand a person reading them, but I can't for the life of me see why people have to write them. (*Gathering them up*) I know what you're going to say, but it's not what you'd call a useful occupation, is it . . . I see in the papers there's a shortage of postmen. (*Putting books on table*) You're very naughty, Sam . . . I sometimes think you only pretend to be poorly, and then, when I leave the room, God only knows what you get up to . . . chair always neatly parked too, just where I left it. . . . (*Trying a desk drawer*) Why d'you always lock everything? (*She picks up a book*) "Encyclopaedia Britannica, Volume Eight" . . . Eight. (*Moving towards bookcase*) Hm . . . Eight, that'll go between Seven and Nine now, won't it. (*She replaces the book on the shelf*) When you've read one, you've read them all, I always say . . . (*Starts shuffling papers on the desk*) What's this, then? All right, all right, I'm not inquisitive, never have been . . . "My Autobiography, Chapter Eight" . . . Hm, not bad, your handwriting, considering your age. . . . (*She reads*) "She knew then that her lover . . ." . . . and so on and so on . . . "Face to face. In spite of her nakedness she felt no . . ." What's this word? . . . Oh, well, you don't change. One thing about old age, though, it does mellow a man . . . Even ten years ago, you'd have blown my head off for as much as glancing at your precious manuscripts. Drink your milk. The radio says there'll be a few bright intervals tomorrow, in spite of a trough of low pressure . . . if it looks at all promising, I might wheel you out for a moment or two . . . On second thoughts, I don't think you really appreciate kindness . . . if you

4

did, you'd be ill in your own bed upstairs like any normal invalid.
I mean, it makes it so difficult for the cleaning woman, this . . .
we'll *lose* Mrs. Spink if we're not careful . . . she's not ideal, but
then who is these days? (*Throwing bits of crumpled manuscript
into the fireplace*) But then, a genius like you has no time to think
about who cleans up behind you and who does all the sordid
things of life, paying the bills . . . you weren't even much of a
father, were you? You were even too busy to tell Tommy the facts
of life, remember? (*Going to the bedside*) He had a perfectly
terrible time at school.

(*Pause.* SAM *makes a sound of irritation*)

You don't remember. How very convenient. And you never
even touched your milk! (*Busily straightening the bedclothes*)
You are, without doubt, the silliest, most stubborn, most childish
old man the world has ever known . . . and it's just impossible
to keep up a normal conversation with you. (*She picks up an
empty medicine glass*) If you need anything, ring the bell like an
ordinary person, don't start shouting. (*She switches off the desk
lamp*) Goodnight, Sam, and sleep well, or whatever it is you do
down here.

(*She kisses him on the forehead and goes out*)

SAM
(*After a pause*)
I enjoyed that chat, Stella . . . thank you very much.
(*He reaches for the glass of milk from the table, makes
as if to drink it, changes his mind and empties it into an ap-
propriate receptacle by the bedside, then turns off the bedside lamp. He chuckles and settles down. Pause. The door
opens and a* MAN *in a dinner jacket comes into the room.
He is about sixty, well groomed, with an elegant beard. He*

5

wears a large carnation in his buttonhole. He crosses fur-
tively to the desk, switches on the desk lamp, and dials a
telephone number. SAM *grunts in his sleep. The* MAN *stops*
dialing and calls. For purposes of identification we will
refer to him as ELDERLY)

ELDERLY

Williams! (*He listens, calls again*) Williams!
  (*There is no sound, so he continues dialing. As soon as*
his number begins to ring, he relaxes slightly. When the re-
ceiver at the other end is taken up, his expression changes
to one of almost embarrassing sweetness)
  Hello? . . . Who do you think it is? Bunny . . . (*With slight*
irritation) Bunny, your Bunny . . . I'm not disguising my voice
. . . your voice sounds quite normal. . . . What? What's the
matter? You're behaving as though you're not alone . . . Mm?
. . . Who is it? . . . A relative? . . . One of those convenient
uncles people have? I have a standby aunt, myself, but then I'm
a man . . . Of course I'm jealous, but I'm more than jealous, I'm
a little annoyed. . . . You realize, I suppose, what time it is . . .
you don't? It's nearly seven-thirty. . . . Exactly, and you're in a
housecoat, I bet, that ruffled pink one with a look of half-
neglected sin about it . . . yes, so that if I hadn't called, I'd have
been round at your place in a quarter of an hour, and found myself alone with your uncle, both of us talking about the weather
while both of us were thinking what the hell's the other doing
here. . . . (*He becomes more positive*) What do I suggest? I
suggest you get rid of your uncle this minute, and come over
here. . . . What? . . . I know it's an unconventional way of doing things, and that the swain should, by tradition, fetch the

6

nymph, but I have a reason, a concrete reason, Clarice, in a flat leather box lined with blue velvet . . . I knew you'd understand . . . No, no, she's still away . . . I just talked to her on the phone to make sure . . . she was very touched that I'd called . . . the weather at Angmering is lovely, and Tommy's getting over his tonsillitis . . . Cook's out . . . I even managed to get rid of Williams . . . the palazzo is empty . . . bless you too, you infidel . . . ten minutes . . . what? All right, if you can't find a taxi, eleven minutes. . . .

(*He hangs up with a smile.* SAM *wakes up, and stares at* ELDERLY. ELDERLY *takes a key out of his pocket, and opens a drawer in the desk, the drawer that* STELLA *had tried to open. He withdraws the flat leather box and opens it. Inside is a diamond necklace.* SAM *sits up.* ELDERLY *replaces it in the drawer with evident satisfaction and anticipation*)

SAM

What are you doing here?

ELDERLY
(*Alarmed*)
I might ask the same of you.

SAM

This is my study.

ELDERLY
How strange. I was under the impression it was mine.

SAM
Don't be ridiculous, I live here.

7

ELDERLY

What a coincidence. So do I.

SAM

There's something about you which is familiar.

ELDERLY

Ah, thank goodness. The spell is broken. I've never seen you before in my life.

SAM

How did you open that drawer?

ELDERLY

With a key.

SAM

I'm the only one to have a key to that drawer.

ELDERLY

So am I.
                  (*Pause. The* TWO MEN *stare at each other*)
Now that we've had our little game, I respectfully suggest you clear out of here, before I call the police.

SAM
                  (*Incredulous*)
What? (*Switches on his bedside lamp*) What do you take me for, a burglar?

8

ELDERLY

It's a rather conventional theory, I admit, but it's the only one that comes to mind.

SAM

Have you ever heard of a burglar breaking into a house in bed?

ELDERLY

No, I haven't. Still, the bed was there. I often work at night. You heard me coming, and hid.

SAM

The bed may have been there, but was the wheelchair? Were these bottles of medicine? You know, it has to be a pretty sick burglar who needs to carry all this paraphernalia with him on every job.
  (*Curious,* ELDERLY *takes a few steps forward*)
  (*Waving his stick at* ELDERLY) Hold your distance, sir. Now, sir, perhaps we may be reasonable. I would be obliged if you called the police, but on my behalf. Would you do that for me, sir? You're nearer the phone than I am, and you must realize I'm none too mobile.

ELDERLY
(*Quietly*)

May I ask your name?

SAM
(*After a pause*)
Are you thinking what I'm thinking? There is something about

9

you that I recognize. A quality of mind. It has prevented me from being really frightened of you.

ELDERLY

I don't believe in this kind of thing, you know.

SAM

What kind of thing?

ELDERLY

There aren't really any words to explain it.

SAM

You're hedging.

ELDERLY

Yes, I am. (*Suddenly*) Would it help if I went?

SAM

Not now, it wouldn't. Not after what's happened.

ELDERLY

What has happened?

SAM

You tell me.

(*Pause*)

ELDERLY
(*Offering* SAM *his case*)

Cigarette?

10

SAM

No, I don't. Gave it up. Doctor's orders.

ELDERLY
(*About to light his cigarette at desk*)
Oh, did it come to that.

SAM

Yes, heart.

ELDERLY
(*Hastily blowing out the flame*)
Heart?

SAM

Apparently.
    (ELDERLY *sits cautiously by desk. He drops the ciga-rette*)
                    (*Pause*)
What's the time?

ELDERLY

Seven-thirty.

SAM

Date?

ELDERLY

The sixteenth.

11

SAM

The sixteenth of what?

ELDERLY

November.

SAM

What year?

ELDERLY

Suppose you tell me.

(*Pause*)

SAM
(*Slowly*)

Where's . . . Stella?

ELDERLY

In Angmering.

SAM

Angmering?

(*He stares in horror*)

ELDERLY

What's the matter?

SAM

Angmering . . .

12

ELDERLY

What is it?

SAM

Has Tommy got over his tonsillitis?

ELDERLY

Yes.

SAM

And is it Cook's day off?

ELDERLY

Yes.

SAM

And did you send Williams to the theatre? Two tickets?

ELDERLY

Now just a minute . . .

SAM

Yes! You've just put down the receiver. You were talking to Clarice. In that drawer you have a diamond necklace you bought for her at Cartier's. It cost you seven thousand pounds. You've hidden the receipt in your driving license. (*Powerfully*) Call her back. Tell her not to come here. Do as I tell you!

ELDERLY

What the devil are you talking about? You're beginning to annoy me.

13

SAM

You're turning sixty, she's twenty-three. You're too old for her. You'll make a fool of yourself.

ELDERLY

I'm in love with the girl!

SAM

Oh, don't be silly! Oh, you maneuvered it all so brilliantly — why, you've only just come down from upstairs where you were phoning Stella, in Angmering. "How are you, my darling? And how's Tommy?" you asked. And then old Williams came up to you afterwards, his head wobbling from side to side as always, and said he couldn't help overhearing, and might he ask how Madam and the young master were. "Well, thank you, Williams," you said. . . . "They'll be back home soon, Thank God."

ELDERLY
(*Tense*)

Go on . . .

SAM

You have booked a table at the Café de Paris for yourself and Clarice, upstairs, where it's dark. Oh . . . you'll have to wait till after eight before she gets here.

ELDERLY

After eight?

SAM

Yes. She'll tell you she had quite a time getting rid of her

14

uncle. Uncle? He's a stockbroker called Schweitzer, Britain's second string on the toboggan team of the Cresta run in 1924. He stutters.

ELDERLY

Why shouldn't I take Clarice out? . . . Even to dinner?

SAM

You know perfectly well it won't end there. Dinner? That's not adultery, is it? But you've got a trump card . . . a valuable necklace. You know perfectly well that Clarice is a hospitable creature who will wish to return your kindness, and since she's not the sort of girl who will present you with a pair of gold cuff-links, she will doubtless do this in a more economical and personal fashion. At any rate, that's what you hope. Oh, incidentally, be prepared for a shock when she eventually comes here.

ELDERLY

Why?

SAM

In order to place that necklace on her person, you will first of all have to remove another one, rather more expensive.

ELDERLY

More expensive!

SAM

Ruby, platinum and pearl. Quite hideous.

15

ELDERLY

Who gave it her? This Schweitzer?

SAM

I knew you'd ask me that. No, someone that neither you nor
Schweitzer had ever heard of — and if you had heard of him,
there was nothing either you or Schweitzer could have done
about it.

ELDERLY

(*Bitterly*)

I suppose she fell in love with someone her own age . . .

SAM

What an incurable romantic you are! Love? Money! Money of
the kind neither you with your best-selling royalties nor Schweitzer
with his single Rolls Royce could ever match. Clarice never fell in
love with anyone, but the Maharaj-Kumar of Khanawala-Pushar
fell in love with her shape, with her equipment. You could never
compete with a Maharajah or for a woman like Clarice . . .

ELDERLY

(*With evident pain*)

Did she marry him?

SAM

Yes, she did. And two years later, she jumped from the twelfth
floor of a New York hotel. That was her only say in the matter.

ELDERLY

How do you know all this?

SAM

I read the newspapers.

(*Pause*)

ELDERLY

Sam.

SAM
(*Smiling*)

Yes, Sam.

ELDERLY

Which one of us is alive?

SAM

Come and help me out of bed, and I'll show you.
(ELDERLY *moves reluctantly towards the bed*)
Come on, don't be frightened. (*Getting out of bed with diffi-culty*) Look at my feet. Do you remember when they used to win us the marathon race? They went faster and faster into the finishing stretch. We never even had to give them a thought, did we? (*Moving slowly to wheelchair, assisted by* ELDERLY) Now I think of little else. They've died before me, Sam, like the teeth, those little tombstones in the mouth that go one by one as a foretaste of oblivion. I'm alive, Sam, but only just.

ELDERLY
(*Horrified*)

Those are my feet?

17

SAM

Do you want them? You can have them if you wish. I don't feel very attached to them. They look like the feet of a twelfth-century monk in a cathedral, don't they? All made of the same block of stone, with a little dust in the crevices to make them look real.

(ELDERLY *walks away towards the desk.* SAM, *now in his chair, wheels himself into the center of the room*)

ELDERLY

What's the phone number here?

SAM

Flaxman 0602. Why?

ELDERLY

It says on the phone it is Kelvin 9658.

SAM

Oh, no, that was changed years ago.
(*They look at one another. Pause*)
You're not serious.

ELDERLY

(*Finding book on desk*)
Here's the latest edition of Who's Who. (*He thumbs rapidly through the pages*) Samuel Barnett Kinsale. Author. Latest work: *Ardent Summer.*

SAM

Oh, come on! — They must mention *Rust on the Armour?*

18

ELDERLY

What's that?

SAM

My last book. It went rather well.

ELDERLY

A book I haven't written yet? Then I'm alive.

SAM

What are you suggesting . . . ? That I'm . . . ? You think I'm joking about these legs? Look!
(*He tries to stand.* ELDERLY *is just in time to catch him*)

ELDERLY
(*Gravely*)

Sam, we are both alive.

SAM

How is that possible?

ELDERLY
(*Slowly*)

I don't know. (*Settles* SAM *in his chair again, and moves away*)
But Clarice is going to come here shortly.

SAM

You're not going to see her, are you?

ELDERLY

I must!

19

SAM

Oh, Sam, you will make a fool of yourself, I promise you that!

ELDERLY

You probably don't remember the kind of physical hunger you
had for her . . . the desire to touch her . . . even gently . . .
the shape of her shoulders, Sam . . . the curve of her neck . . .

SAM

No, I don't remember any of that . . . I don't even remember
the color of her eyes . . . they were a kind of watery blue,
weren't they?

ELDERLY

No. Dark brown . . . they change miraculously according to
the clothes she wears.

SAM

Do they really? I don't remember that. I remember lying in
bed beside her . . . well, you know . . . and I do remember not
feeling terribly well myself. I got a kind of stitch. And I remember
thinking how idiotic it was that a man who used to win the marathon race should suffer from a stitch, of all things. I remember
getting dressed with difficulty, it was hideously embarrassing.
Then I had to take a taxi home. I gave the driver a pound, no five
pounds, God knows how much it was. In any case, after spending
seven thousand pounds on a necklace, what difference did it
make? I had to call the doctor. I told him I thought I'd been over-
doing it a bit. I don't know whether he understood what I was
driving at. At all events he gave me an electric cardiphone, whatever they call it . . . the heart had gone, the heart of a twenty-

six-miler. Stella came back from Angmering, and looked after me like a lamb. I took all my medicines without a murmur, as a penance. There was peace in the house . . . for about a week.

ELDERLY
(*Cautiously*)

How is Stella?

SAM

Oh . . . friends tell me she's a wonderful person. I'm afraid I'm the last one to judge. . . .

ELDERLY

Well, after all, you are her husband.

SAM
(*Moving away*)

No cynicism, Sam. I'm too old. I've half given it up.

ELDERLY

I'm sorry.

SAM

Oh, for heaven's sake don't apologize. Just tell me you're not going to go through with this Clarice nonsense.

ELDERLY

Yes, I am.

SAM

On the assumption it's going to work out differently this time?

21

ELDERLY

No, I believe you. I think exactly the same thing is going to happen. I don't feel terribly well at the moment as a matter of fact. Keep taking deep breaths.

SAM

Well then, Sam?

ELDERLY

You forget, I'm in love with the woman.

SAM

Oh, don't be such an ass!

ELDERLY

I don't care. I must go through with this.

SAM

Are you being quite fair to Stella?

ELDERLY

That's hitting below the belt.

SAM

Only sensible place to hit you.

ELDERLY

Well, are you being quite fair to Stella? You can talk.

SAM

That evens the score.

22

(A MAN's *voice can be heard shouting in the corridor.*
SAM *and* ELDERLY *become conscious of it; a distant* WOMAN's
voice answers the MAN's *offstage*)

VOICE

You understand absolutely nothing about me, my work, or anything artistic . . . That, if I may say so, is a typical woman's remark.

(ELDERLY *moves away to conceal himself in the window
bay,* SAM *backs away to below the bed*)

If you had your way, I'd be writing a safe sentimental piece for
a woman's magazine, or better still working in a bank with regular hours and a regular pay check . . . Thank God, I didn't hear
that last remark . . . all right, go away, go away . . . Shut up!
Once and for all, shut your damned mouth!

(A MAN *in the flower of middle age enters. His hair is
tousled. He wears a short beard. He is in tweeds. He strides
into the center of the room, seeing neither* ELDERLY, *who has
retired into the shadows, nor* SAM, *who is in darkness at the
foot of the bed. We will call the newcomer* MIDDLE-AGED)

MIDDLE-AGED

I can't stand it a moment longer. Not one damned moment
longer. (*In a sudden tantrum, he picks up a china ornament from
the desk, and smashes it into the fireplace. He looks up at the ceiling*) There. I hope you heard that. Yes, it belonged to your father.
So goddamned phlegmatic and cool, aren't you, so self-contained,
such a little lady, with your public smile and your crooked finger
holding the teacup and that Niagara of small talk? Well, I'll give
you something to be cool about. (*He crosses to the desk, sits
down, searches for a key in his waistcoat, and opens the notorious*

23

drawer. He pulls out a framed photograph, which he looks at amorously, then kisses passionately) Oh, Miriam . . .

(ELDERLY *and* SAM *emit small moans.* ELDERLY *approaches from the shadows, and looks over* MIDDLE-AGED'S *shoulder, pain written on his face. With a defiant glance at the door,* MIDDLE-AGED *places the photograph firmly on the desk. He takes out a pen, and begins to write, seeking inspiration from the face before him.* ELDERLY *reads over his shoulder, then looks up and stares at* SAM, *who stares back. With a sudden decision,* ELDERLY *goes upstage, turns on the lights, and locks the door.*)

MIDDLE-AGED
(*Rising, shocked*)

Who are you?

ELDERLY

You're running an absurd risk with that photograph on the desk and the door unlocked.

MIDDLE-AGED

I don't care if she does come in. Who are you, anyway?

ELDERLY

Don't be afraid. I know all about it. Sit down. No, I'm not a burglar. My name's Sam Kinsale.

MIDDLE-AGED

Oh?

ELDERLY

Isn't that your name too?

24

MIDDLE-AGED

Yes.

ELDERLY

I thought so. We've been through it all.

MIDDLE-AGED

We?

SAM

We. Us. Sam, Sam and Sam. Sounds like a firm of corrupt lawyers, doesn't it?

MIDDLE-AGED

You're another one?

SAM

We're all the same one.
            (*He wheels himself center*)

ELDERLY

You're beginning to wonder what institution we've escaped from.

MIDDLE-AGED

I'm beginning to wonder what institution we're in.

ELDERLY

You took it better than I did. That's because you're younger. How old are you?

25

MIDDLE-AGED

Forty. Forty today. That row was a birthday present from my wife.

ELDERLY

Stella.

MIDDLE-AGED

You know her?

ELDERLY

I've known her longer than you have.

SAM

I know her vaguely, too.
          (SAM *and* ELDERLY *chuckle together*)

MIDDLE-AGED
(*Sitting again*)

Now suppose you let me into the secret. I mean, I'm a good sport, I can laugh at myself, I've trained myself to — but I find it awfully hard to laugh unless it's made fairly clear to me why I'm supposed to.

SAM

No one's asking you to laugh. That's up to your natural inclination.

MIDDLE-AGED

My natural inclination is to summon the police.

26

ELDERLY

(*Laughing*)

That was our natural inclination too, when we first saw each other. (*He looks at the photograph*) My God, she was a good looker, Miriam.

SAM

Who's that?

ELDERLY

Miriam.

SAM

Ah, Miriam! I was thinking only yesterday at breakfast that she was the only woman I ever really loved.

(SAM *takes the photograph from* ELDERLY. MIDDLE-AGED *suddenly seizes it back*)

Oh, why are you so possessive about her?

MIDDLE-AGED

Why should you look at Miriam?

SAM

Because I remember her with a great autumnal sorrow.

(*Whistles and rattles are heard in the distance*)

ELDERLY

What's that?

MIDDLE-AGED

The air-raid warning.

27

ELDERLY

The air-raid warning? Oh, of course, if you're only forty . . .

MIDDLE-AGED

Stella's frightened. She'll be down here in a minute.

ELDERLY

(*Taking the photograph from* MIDDLE-AGED)
No, she won't be.

MIDDLE-AGED

How d'you know?

ELDERLY

Because I remember. She was so angry with you, she conquered her fear, and managed to sit it out in the bedroom. Afterwards she gave you hell for not being gallant enough to go up and fetch her in spite of the fact that the Zeppelin warning had sounded. "You don't care if I die" she said, and you were honest enough to remain silent.

SAM

Oh, my God.

ELDERLY

What?

SAM

Yes, I remember that too, now. I remember being quite grateful for the war. There was always the chance the enemy would carry out your death wish for you.

28

MIDDLE-AGED
(*Sitting at the desk*)
You mean you can read my mind like that?

SAM
It's our mind, Sam, it's our mind. But I've got bad news for you.
Stella survives the war.

MIDDLE-AGED
(*Guiltily*)
I never really wanted her to die.

SAM
Oh, yes you did. Coldly and dispassionately. It was quite a relief to have such a tidy mind about it. It was quite a relief to
know what you wanted, without doubt — with a little guilt on occasion, but without doubt.

MIDDLE-AGED
You can't really blame Stella.

SAM
Ah, the perfect gentleman. Remind me why you can't blame
Stella.

MIDDLE-AGED
Every woman should be a mother. She's built for it.

SAM
Oh yes . . .

29

MIDDLE-AGED

For some reason, it hasn't worked between us. I don't know . . .
perhaps I should see a doctor . . . I know I should . . . but I
keep avoiding it. I so loathe that avuncular atmosphere which
surrounds confessions of the kind I'd be forced to make . . . the
vague smell of ether . . . and the feeling that the nurse is listen-
ing behind the door. Stella's been to see him, and she says he's
waiting to see me, but I keep putting it off. She says pointedly
that he's examined her, and that she's all right.

SAM

Well, now I have some good news for you. You do have a child.

MIDDLE-AGED

From Stella?

SAM

Oh, yes.

MIDDLE-AGED
(*Violent*)

That's not good news! I don't want a child from Stella. I've
made up my mind to leave her! Tonight, I made it up. I'm going
to make a fresh start with Miriam.

ELDERLY

You're too late . . .

MIDDLE-AGED

Too late? That's a lie. You mean Miriam has gone off with
someone else? You don't know the girl. She's the only person I've

30

ever felt really happy with . . . and relaxed . . . The only person who understands my work, what I'm trying to do, without always thinking of success, success, public acceptance, the rest of it. And d'you know why it works? Because I brought a little light and gaiety into her life. I like myself in her presence. I'm fun. I'm witty. I glow!

ELDERLY

That's all quite true, Sam, but you're still too late. Stella's pregnant at this moment.

MIDDLE-AGED

That's ridiculous. Why she'd be the first one to tell me if it were true!

ELDERLY

She doesn't know herself yet.

MIDDLE-AGED

What?

(*Pause*)

ELDERLY

(*Somber*)

Yes, it happened after one of your many reconciliations . . . (*He sits at the desk*) Some six or seven weeks ago . . . you had the mother of all rows, remember? . . . She was in tears, so were you . . . it all seemed suddenly so hopeless, you were almost inclined to laugh, both of you . . . there was a sudden silence after all the shouting . . . you both felt so lonely, you made love al-

31

most without thinking . . . you were so relaxed, so weak, so neg-
ligent, it worked . . . Tommy's on his way.

MIDDLE-AGED

Tommy? I don't even like the name.

ELDERLY

It's Stella's favorite.

MIDDLE-AGED

And . . . Miriam?

SAM

Oh . . . the only true love is the unconsummated one . . . the
dream. I remember to this day the divine candor of her expression, like a window open on the truth . . . Oh, Miriam. (*Pause*)
What ever happened to her?

MIDDLE-AGED
(*Violent*)

You mean you don't even know?

SAM
(*Embarrassed*)

Well, I'm eighty.

ELDERLY

She married a Dr. Dixon Lawrie or Lawrence.

MIDDLE-AGED

Who?

32

ELDERLY

A Canadian, I think he was, or South African.

SAM

A Canadian, yes. Some Canadian from . . . Canada.

ELDERLY

It didn't work very well. I got rather a pathetic Christmas card from somewhere abroad . . . oh, quite recently. She must be fifty-two or -three.

SAM
(*Nodding*)

Seventy-three.

MIDDLE-AGED
(*After a pause*)

There's nothing you can do about it. I'm going to leave Stella.

ELDERLY

Oh, I know you are. You get as far as the Regent Palace Hotel. You stay the night. Then you're back in the morning. She's seeing Dr. Brackett at three o'clock. She'll tell you at half-past four. You'll open a bottle of champagne over supper . . . to celebrate.

SAM

What's the time?

ELDERLY

Ten to eight. (*Rises*) Any minute now.

33

MIDDLE-AGED

What are we waiting for?

ELDERLY

Clarice Donohue.

MIDDLE-AGED

Who?

ELDERLY

You haven't met her yet. But when you do . . .

MIDDLE-AGED

Who's she?

ELDERLY

A girl. Oh, not a mind, not a kindred spirit, I don't think she's
ever learned to read. Just a body. A receptacle for a man's passion.

MIDDLE-AGED

How revolting you've become.

ELDERLY

Yes, but it's so uncomplicated, so relaxing not to have to exer-
cise the spirit all the time.

MIDDLE-AGED

You've made concessions, haven't you, all the way down the
line.

ELDERLY

Concessions? To what and from what? That's the kind of expression earnest students use. You never made a concession, did you, and look at the result. Books which sell eight hundred copies with luck. After every failure you drift closer to Miriam . . . you two are closer and more alone against the world . . . what was the phrase you used? You're more fun, wittier, aglow. And where's the glory in it? Every time the critics call your work incomprehensible, the two of you exult in the loneliness of it all, in recognition after death, all the rancid consolations of the immature. And meanwhile, you subsist on father's inheritance in this mid-Victorian barn, with three servants paid for with the profits of a coal mine. What kind of integrity is that?

MIDDLE-AGED
(*Furious*)
Did you have the guts to move out of the family mansion?

ELDERLY

I had no more guts than you, since we're the same person. At least I began to write like someone who lives in a house of this kind. I pleased the public. And I made money!

MIDDLE-AGED

Do the critics praise you now?

ELDERLY

Now they ignore me. They don't need me and I don't need them. I have a direct appeal to a million charwomen, office workers and elderly spinsters. I don't need to sport a dirty beard to show people I'm an artist. I don't need to have filthy fingernails.

(MIDDLE-AGED *glances at his nails, and puts his hands in his pockets*)

— Yes, I saw them, I'm not protesting about anything. I'm not happy! Who is? But I'm content.

MIDDLE-AGED

You're not only content, you're self-satisfied . . . Content? Is that the function of a writer to be content? Can a man write at all if he's content? I never thought that when I was sixty I'd be the kind of empty shell in a beautifully pressed dinner jacket who'd be waiting to take blondes dancing, vertically first, then later, horizontally. I may have a dirty beard, but what's that moribund carnation supposed to symbolize? The flower of your manhood fluttering from your masthead like a pirate flag? And what's that smell? Cologne for men, to drown the odors of tobacco, toil and premature decay. And what's that stuff on your hair?

ELDERLY

Eau de Portugal.

MIDDLE-AGED

Eau de Portugal. (*Catching* ELDERLY's *hand*) You don't have filthy nails, each one of yours is like a miniature skating rink, cuticles pushed back like surplus snow at the edges. I say, it must be fun having them done, isn't it? There's something backhandedly sexy about having your fingers held by a scented girl, and then letting them dangle afterwards in a luke-warm bath. It's as though each finger was a little Casanova on its own, with an independent life and independent pleasures.

(ELDERLY *moves away*)

I'm not being pompous; I'd just like to know, for my own information . . . Can you afford it?

(ELDERLY *opens his mouth to reply*)

Oh, I'm sorry, I don't mean financially. I mean physically. Morally. Is there a real sense of contentment in feeling the warmth of a whore's body next to yours? Are you always sure that her closed eyelids conceal tender thoughts of you? Haven't you perhaps been overcharged in attaining your particular square inch of paradise?

ELDERLY

I wish you'd stop it. (*Pause*) I don't like myself any more than you do . . . there was a kind of tact about your anger which hurt more than anything you said . . . Why didn't you mention how fat I had become?

MIDDLE-AGED

Perhaps because it was that that shocked me most . . . Do you realize that you used to be a runner?

ELDERLY

I've let myself go . . . and when a man does that, he blames it on the world . . . if he hates his life, he says that life is like that. Oh, I'm honest on occasions . . . that's why I suffer.

MIDDLE-AGED

Then tell me the truth. I can't believe a day will come when I will no longer think of Miriam.

37

ELDERLY

What you can't have, you kill. I killed her memory because your cowardice made me do it.

MIDDLE-AGED

My cowardice! What the hell do you mean?

ELDERLY

Cowardice! If you'd. . . .

SAM

Stop it, both of you! You're as cruel towards one another as only brothers can be . . . and you're the same man . . . me! Don't you realize I carry both your tragedies within myself?

ELDERLY

No self-pity now, Sam. That's something we've all been prone to.

SAM

Oh, you're very cruel. It's all right for you two. You only have the past to worry about. What about the future? You know that you don't die soon . . . my presence here is a guarantee of that. I have no such consolation.

MIDDLE-AGED
(*Moving away*)
Death never frightened me.

SAM

What?

38

MIDDLE-AGED

You told me that I sometimes wished for Stella's death. Not really. I wished her no harm. She has qualities. I just don't happen to like them. All I really want is a solution. I'm almost ready to die myself.

ELDERLY

Hm . . . almost.

MIDDLE-AGED

What do you mean by that?

ELDERLY

What do you mean by that? If a bomb should fall, you'd rather it was on Stella.

MIDDLE-AGED

I've sometimes prayed for a bomb to fall on both of us.

ELDERLY

And at other times, you've hoped for a bomb to fall on Stella.

MIDDLE-AGED
(*After a pause*)
It's terrible to have no secrets.
(*Sits at desk*)

ELDERLY

Isn't it?

39

MIDDLE-AGED

It makes conversation impossible.

ELDERLY

It also makes you feel a frightful bastard.
(*Pause*)

SAM

(*Moving center with a sudden burst of laughter*)
Well, *I* have secrets though. I've got twenty years of secrets.

ELDERLY

You can't cheat us.

SAM

I think I could if I put my mind to it — but I don't really want
to. Oh, I think of Miriam with a haunting regret, if that helps you
. . . not very often, I'm afraid, but I do sometimes think of her. I
never think of Clarice at all.

ELDERLY

I'm not a bit surprised.

SAM

Mainly, I'm afraid, I think of myself, as though when you're old,
selfishness is really all that's left to you. There are compensations,
of course. I am rather better known than either of you were. I
managed to avoid the obscurity of your style, Sam . . . and the
frivolity of yours, Sam. I found one of my own which is not
devoid of profundity, if I do say so myself. We're often reprinted
even in quite the most advanced literary magazines.

40

(MIDDLE-AGED *and* ELDERLY *look at one another*)
I thought that would please you both.

(*He grows grave*)

What may please you less is that you live out your life with Stella to an end which is not particularly bitter . . . it's often quite amusing, not to me, probably not to her either, but it would be to an observer, if there was one . . . she's upstairs now, sitting on our double bed, her hair in curlers, without a thought in her head . . . (*He smiles wanly*) It's not often that winter has the opportunity to compare notes with summer, and with autumn . . .

(ELDERLY *looks at his watch*)

What's the time, autumn?

ELDERLY

A minute to go.

SAM

There's only one presence I fear more than Clarice Donohue at this moment.

ELDERLY

Who's that?

SAM

Spring. The missing season. (*To* MIDDLE-AGED) I don't think I could face myself any younger than you.

ELDERLY

Nor could I.

41

MIDDLE-AGED
(*Rises*)
I'm leaving anyway. I've made up my mind —
(*He is interrupted by the sound of laughter and voices outside*)

SAM
What's up?

MIDDLE-AGED
There are voices in the corridor . . .

SAM
Oh no . . . I don't want voices in the corridor.

ELDERLY
That's impossible. The house is empty. I sent Williams away.

MIDDLE-AGED
It may be Nanny.

ELDERLY
Nanny died last year.
(MIDDLE-AGED, ELDERLY *and* SAM *withdraw into the shadows. The door opens and a* YOUNG MAN *in plus-fours enters, with a very pretty* GIRL *dressed in the clothes of the late-Victorian period. Daylight seeps through the curtains*)

YOUNG MAN
In here . . . Come on, don't be frightened. This is Daddy's study. Isn't it grim?

42

GIRL

Yes. (*Looking at things on the desk*) Is it all right to . . . ?

YOUNG MAN

Oh, he never comes in here at this hour. We're quite safe. Now for the wonderful news I told you about. My book of poems.

GIRL

Yes?

YOUNG MAN

I got a letter from the Partridge Press this morning. They're going to publish them!

GIRL

Oh Sam! Sam . . . darling . . .

YOUNG MAN

(*Who has already half-forgotten the poems, looks deep into the girl's eyes*)
Oh, Stella, I love you . . .
(*He kisses her. She melts to his embrace.* ELDERLY *stands still, like a man in mourning.* MIDDLE-AGED *seems to wish to shout, to express his agony.* SAM *groans, and turns away*)

SAM

No! . . .

CURTAIN

43

Act Two

ACT TWO

SAM *is back in bed.* ELDERLY *is sitting on a footstool by the bed, with* MIDDLE-AGED *standing behind him.* YOUNG *is leaning against the desk.*

ELDERLY
(*Sternly*)
Sam, you're play-acting. I know you. You think you want to die from shock. You don't really.

MIDDLE-AGED
Oh, let him die.

ELDERLY
It's all very well for you. You're in the first gloom of middle age. We all think we're near the end as we get near forty. Our lives seem meaningless. Have a little consideration for those who've got their second wind. Clarice will be here at any moment. If he dies, I presume we die too, and I desperately don't want to die. I've just spent seven thousand on a necklace.

MIDDLE-AGED
How much?

ELDERLY
Seven thousand pounds.

47

MIDDLE-AGED
(*Whistles*)
Your books must be selling well.

ELDERLY
The last one has just gone into its eighteenth printing.

MIDDLE-AGED
That's an enormous concession.

ELDERLY
Enormous. Now Sam, Sam . . . be reasonable.

YOUNG
I wonder how many copies my poems will sell.

MIDDLE-AGED
Eighteen. Eleven of them to libraries, the rest to relatives.

YOUNG
Well that's something. It's a start.

MIDDLE-AGED
They're not bad, those poems.

YOUNG
You think so?

MIDDLE-AGED
They have a freshness, an awkwardness.

48

YOUNG

After all, I'm only twenty.

MIDDLE-AGED

That's true. Mustn't forget that. In fact that's 100 per cent of their charm. They're full of ill-digested and rather obvious symbolism.

YOUNG
(*Hotly*)

Obvious. Not at all. I flatter myself they're very hard to understand.

ELDERLY
(*To them*)

Please spare us this literary salon. (*To* SAM) Sam! Sam!

YOUNG
(*Sitting in wheelchair*)

I wonder how this wheelchair works. Now that I know I'll be in it eventually I might as well get used to it.
(*He propels the chair around rapidly*)

SAM
(*Sitting up violently*)

Leave that alone! It's not a toy. That's my only means of conveyance! Put it back where it belongs.
(YOUNG *wheels the chair away to below the bed*)

49

ELDERLY
(*Drily*)

Thank you, young man. (*The doorbell rings. Rising*) Oh,
Lord. That's Clarice. Make yourself scarce.

MIDDLE-AGED

Why? I'd rather like to watch.

ELDERLY

She'll see you! Be a sport, and leave me alone with her. I can't
function if I feel I'm being watched. Sam, cover yourself up with
your blankets, and for God's sake don't listen. How do I look?

MIDDLE-AGED

Immaculate. Like an advertisement for hair cream.

ELDERLY

Clothes all right?

MIDDLE-AGED

Not a crease in them. You might have walked straight out of a
shop window.
(*The bell rings again, insistently*)

ELDERLY

Please help me.
(*He goes*)

YOUNG
(*To* SAM)

Who's Clarice?

50

SAM

What?

YOUNG

Clarice.

SAM

Shut up, and hide.

YOUNG

But where's Stella? Don't I marry her?

MIDDLE-AGED

You most certainly do. Come on.

YOUNG

But I don't understand!

SAM

You're not supposed to! You're the youngest.
(MIDDLE-AGED *pulls* YOUNG *into the shadows, and* SAM *covers himself with blankets as giggles are heard in the hallway.* ELDERLY *enters with* CLARICE, *a very obvious blonde, blonder, in fact, than she was born*)

ELDERLY

Clarice! (*He kisses her bare shoulder.* CLARICE *expresses conventional ecstasy. He recoils as he notices her ruby necklace*) Where did you get this necklace?

51

CLARICE

Oh, I have an absurdly generous . . . em . . .

ELDERLY

Uncle?

CLARICE

He's more a great-uncle really. They're not all real.

ELDERLY

What, those pearls and rubies?

CLARICE

Yes, some of them are real. Others are just paste, or glass, or something.

ELDERLY

Clarice, you're such a bad liar.

CLARICE

What?

ELDERLY

What kind of jeweler would mix paste and glass with real rubies and pearls?

CLARICE

Well, I don't know anything about jewelry really. Don't care for it very much. It's the spirit in which a gift is given that's important, I always think.

ELDERLY

You might have saved me a lot of money if you'd said that a day or two earlier.

CLARICE

(*Laughs*)

That's what I like about you, you're a cynic. I like cynical people.

ELDERLY

Oh, come, Clarice, you don't even know what a cynic is.

CLARICE

I do! A man of the world. A man who sees things for what they are. I can't bear men who put me on a pedestal, think of me as something special. I'm not special, just a girl, and I like having a good time, without complications. That's why I can't stand young men, why I go for the older type of man, who knows what's what.

ELDERLY

Is that supposed to be a compliment?

CLARICE

Take it as you wish.

(ELDERLY *moves towards her*)

Bunny! (*She touches his lips affectionately with a languorous finger*)

ELDERLY

(*In a hushed, amorous voice*)

Tonight I feel absurdly young, Clarice.

(*Puts his arms round her*)

53

CLARICE

Oh, well . . . that's the best of both worlds, isn't it?

ELDERLY

(*Lifting his head*)

May I take that necklace off, Clarice, it's beginning to annoy me.

CLARICE

Annoy you? Why?

ELDERLY

I don't want another man's passion staring me in the face. A richer man's.

CLARICE

I never think of it like that.

ELDERLY

Well I do. You can afford to be wide-eyed about it. You have no rival. I have. Who could buy a thing like that? It could only be an oil man or a Maharajah.

CLARICE

(*Starting*)

Sam, you're uncanny. . . .

ELDERLY

Why?

54

CLARICE

It is a Meerajah — I never know how to pronounce that word.

ELDERLY

I'm not sure I'm going to help you. Where did you meet him?

CLARICE

In Bond Street, shopping. I only saw him for five minutes. On the pavement.

ELDERLY

On the pavement? And he gave you the necklace there and then?

CLARICE

No, he sent it round to my flat, with the funniest card. He says he's in love with me. You've never read such flowery language.

ELDERLY

Oh, and you had the time and inclination in five minutes to give him your address?

CLARICE
(*With a trace of annoyance*)

Sam, I came here to have fun, not to have dinner with Sherlock Holmes.

ELDERLY

Do you blame me for being jealous?

55

CLARICE

Yes, you ought to trust me. He's ridiculous. Only five foot tall, and very stout. He's definitely not my type.

ELDERLY

May I take it off then?

CLARICE

Yes, take it off, take it off.
(ELDERLY *moves across to undo the necklace*)
It was stupid of me to wear it at all. It's just silly me showing off.

ELDERLY

(*Caressing her neck, the necklace now in his hand*)
I don't know how your pretty neck can bear the weight of this monstrosity.

CLARICE

I do have a slight headache. Maybe it's the necklace.

ELDERLY

Yes. There are ugly welts . . . round the back of your neck.

CLARICE

Oh Sam, how beastly.

ELDERLY

Now, I have a scheme to cover them.
(*He crosses to the desk, takes out his key and opens the*

56

drawer, takes out his case and hands it to her. She opens it and takes out the necklace)

CLARICE

Sam . . . it's beautiful. . . . So much simpler than the other one . . . more tasteful . . . more classical.

ELDERLY

I think so.

CLARICE

Oh, what a lark! They both came from the same shop!

ELDERLY
(Sullen)

Yes, that's very amusing.

CLARICE
(Putting on the necklace)

Carter's.

ELDERLY

Cartier's.

CLARICE

Oh, yes, there's an "i" in it. That's French, is it?

ELDERLY
(Moving to help CLARICE *with the necklace)*
While we're on the subject, I have a table at the Café de Paris.

57

CLARICE

Sam, we won't run into any of your friends there, will we? I mean, I can't afford a scandal.

ELDERLY

I've talked to M. Maurice. We've got a table upstairs, where the lights are low.

CLARICE

Oh, Sam . . .

ELDERLY

And then afterwards. Who knows?

CLARICE

You're wicked.

ELDERLY

It's a delicious sensation. (*He moves to kiss her, but she eludes him*) Aren't you going to thank me for the necklace?

CLARICE

Oh darling, forgive me.
(*He goes to her, and they kiss.* ELDERLY *is more ambitious in his kiss than* CLARICE *will allow him to be*)
Oh, that reminds me. (*She returns to the desk, pops the Maharajah's necklace into the case, collects her handbag and goes through the door which* ELDERLY *is holding open for her*) Bunny! Come on, sweetheart.
(ELDERLY *looks round the room anxiously.* SAM *looks out from under the covers — tells* ELDERLY *in dumb show what an imbecile he is.* ELDERLY *shrugs his shoulders philosophically and follows* CLARICE *out*)

MIDDLE-AGED
(*Breaking cover. Emotional*)
It's hideously embarrassing!

SAM
What are you going to do about it?
(MIDDLE-AGED *picks up the photo of* MIRIAM *which has been standing on the desk with its back to us*)

MIDDLE-AGED
I'm leaving. I'm going to prevent that from ever happening to me. Why, hasn't the man the intelligence to realize what kind of girl that is? . . . What's her name, Clarice? Even the name is horrible.
(*He places the photo in the drawer, and locks it. Returns the key to his waistcoat pocket*)

SAM
Of course he knows. But something inside him died when you hadn't the strength to make a clean break.

MIDDLE-AGED
Are you blaming me for his behavior now?

SAM
Yes, I am. I'm blaming myself and you. Without for a moment knowing what the alternative is.

MIDDLE-AGED
The alternative is to have the courage to obey your heart.

59

SAM

Fine words.

YOUNG

(*To* SAM)

But where's Stella in all this?

MIDDLE-AGED *and* SAM

Upstairs.

YOUNG

Well I do have the courage to obey my heart. I'm going to marry Stella!

MIDDLE-AGED *and* SAM

Shut up!

YOUNG

Why should I?

SAM

Don't involve yourself in things you're too young to understand.

MIDDLE-AGED

That's right. Keep your ears open, you may learn something. Sam, I'm going to leave Stella.

YOUNG

(*Sentimentally*)

You can't! I've only just asked her to marry me.

60

SAM

You're an idiot. (*To* MIDDLE-AGED) You know, it's all his fault, when you come to analyze it.

YOUNG

I'm in love with her!

MIDDLE-AGED

You're too young to know what love is.

YOUNG

You're only young once.

MIDDLE-AGED

Once too often.
(*A female voice, off, calls: "Sam!"*)

SAM

Oh, I'm glad you hid that photograph.

MIDDLE-AGED

Why? Is she going to come in?

SAM
(*Urgently to* YOUNG)
Yes, you'd better hide again.
(YOUNG *withdraws nervously into the shadows.* MIDDLE-AGED *sits at the desk. The door opens, and* STELLA *enters. She is in her late thirties. She is in a nightdress. Her hair is unkempt. She seems no longer to care. She is not ugly, but does her best to make herself so, unsuccessfully*)

61

STELLA MIDDLE-AGED

There's just one thing I want to put on record, Sam. I suppose we can't help having rows . . . we're different in a sense . . . our backgrounds are different, our sense of values . . . we even have different friends . . . you call mine conventional, I call yours dirty and unsuccessful . . . That can't be helped . . . it's unfortunate but it can't be helped . . . but we are married and the marriage vows do entail certain responsibilities . . . you know perfectly well that I'm scared to death of the Zeppelins . . . the warning went over half an hour ago . . . and yet you were heartless enough to leave me alone in our room without making the slightest gesture towards me . . . You don't care if I die up there . . . you wish it.

MIDDLE-AGED

Have you heard a single bomb fall?

STELLA MIDDLE-AGED
(*Moving to desk*)

That is neither here nor there. The point is that the warning has sounded. The first bomb may be the one which will wipe me out.

MIDDLE-AGED

Oh, you wish me to go upstairs in order to share your fate, is that it? Like Romeo and Juliet, you wish us to consummate our rancid love-story with fire and unnecessary death, is that it? (*Rising*) It's absurd to sit up on the second floor during an air-raid, Stella. That's asking for trouble. You're not an invalid, are you? You can walk. What's to prevent you from coming downstairs like any rational person? You've just done so in fact — not to escape the bombs, however, because there are none — but in order to destroy my peace of mind. Well, come along, Stella. Let's go upstairs.

STELLA MIDDLE-AGED
(*Tearfully*)

It's too late, Sam . . . you had your chance . . . you didn't even make a gesture . . .

MIDDLE-AGED

Why? Because it would have been uncharitable of me to go up to you in any case . . . you felt so deliciously misunderstood, so heinously betrayed up there . . . If I'd have gone up, I'd have stolen your favorite pastime, a good cry. You love being wronged, you're never happier than when you see in me an enemy!

STELLA MIDDLE-AGED

I gave you my youth, my health . . .

MIDDLE-AGED

Stick to the point!

STELLA MIDDLE-AGED
(*Emotional*)

Look at me! Am I desirable? I was pretty when I married you — people even said I was beautiful.

MIDDLE-AGED

What of it?

63

STELLA MIDDLE-AGED

(*Turning* MIDDLE-AGED *round to face her*)
Look at me!

MIDDLE-AGED

Is it my fault that you refuse to wear lipstick, that you never go to the hairdresser, that you stay in your dressing gown all day long?

STELLA MIDDLE-AGED

Of course! What's the point of being beautiful?

MIDDLE-AGED

What's the point of writing? What's the point of anything? You tell me my books are out of touch with ordinary people, you tell me they're esoteric, snobbish, dull. You give me no encouragement, no incentive, but I still write. Why do I do it?

STELLA MIDDLE-AGED

I never said your books are esoteric. (*Which she pronounces ee-soteric*)

MIDDLE-AGED

Only because you don't know what it means. It's a good word for the future, however. It expresses exactly what you wish to express, without being too unpleasant. *Esoteric*.

STELLA MIDDLE-AGED

I think you could do better.

64

MIDDLE-AGED

Couldn't you?

STELLA MIDDLE-AGED

I do the best I can. And what thanks do I get? I come
down —

(*A bugle sounds the All-Clear*)

MIDDLE-AGED
(*Opening the curtains*)
There. The All-Clear. There's no point in going back to your
room now. There'll be no bombs tonight.

STELLA MIDDLE-AGED
(*With calm hatred*)
You have all the luck, don't you?

MIDDLE-AGED

What? Oh, I'm responsible for the All-Clear now. The entire
Civil Defense organization is in my pay, and it sounded the All-
Clear not so that ten million people could emerge from shelter
but so that you might suffer a moment of humiliation.

STELLA MIDDLE-AGED

You have a wicked tongue.

MIDDLE-AGED

Not with other people. I'm generally liked.

65

STELLA MIDDLE-AGED

Ha! By those ne'er-do-wells you frequent. They're just about your level.

MIDDLE-AGED

Sycophants is the word you're looking for.

STELLA MIDDLE-AGED

Not normal flesh and blood people with ordinary everyday problems . . . no, bitter, unnatural creatures, who've never done an honest day's work in their lives.

MIDDLE-AGED

Oh?

STELLA MIDDLE-AGED

Yes, and you're one of them. Why, you can't even give me a child.

(*For a moment,* MIDDLE-AGED *seems on the verge of explosion. He controls himself.* STELLA *continues, quite coldly. She has the gift of cruelty, too*)

I've done my duty. I've seen Dr. Brackett. He even sent me to a specialist. I was examined twice, no, three times. It was most unpleasant. There's nothing wrong with me. "Tell your husband to give me a ring," said Dr. Brackett. I promised you would, you promised you would — have you? Oh, dear me no. You're too frightened to be found out for what you are.

MIDDLE-AGED

And what is that?

66

STELLA MIDDLE-AGED

Impotent.

MIDDLE-AGED
(*Smiles. He is quite calm*)
Stella, it is practically impossible to have a child by a person
you detest.

STELLA MIDDLE-AGED

Did you detest me from the beginning? Be honest.

MIDDLE-AGED
(*Sitting at the desk*)
At the beginning you didn't know how to make love. You were
all flushed with the prejudices of the prep school and the whis-
pered fears of the dormitory. You used to grunt and groan in my
arms like a small wart hog. Whenever you said anything it was
"No, no, no."

STELLA MIDDLE-AGED

You succeeded in making half a woman of me. Congratulations.
All the same, it might have been kinder to leave me as I was.

MIDDLE-AGED
(*After a pause*)
I'm convinced that it's kinder to leave you in any condition.

STELLA MIDDLE-AGED
(*After a pause*)
What do you mean by that?

67

MIDDLE-AGED

I have no need to go to see Dr. Brackett. There's nothing he can tell me that I don't know already. I'm even ready to believe I am impotent. With you.

STELLA MIDDLE-AGED

Why don't you leave me?

MIDDLE-AGED

That is precisely what I intend to do.

STELLA MIDDLE-AGED
(*After a pause*)

When?

MIDDLE-AGED

Tonight.

STELLA MIDDLE-AGED
(*After a pause*)

Don't forget your toothbrush.

MIDDLE-AGED

You don't believe me?

STELLA MIDDLE-AGED
(*Smiling, almost affectionately*)

I don't know. Perhaps you're right. I don't know if you can leave me. I don't know how you'll survive without the regular meals, without the laundry, without having the messes you leave tidied up behind you, without these blistering rooms even. You'll miss them.

68

MIDDLE-AGED
(*Smiling*)

You're not clever, Stella, but you have a clever instinct, a woman's instinct. Imperceptibly you've switched on the charm, just a rationed glimpse so I can see a shade of what I first saw in you. But it's too late. My relief at taking this decision is stronger than anything you can do.

(*Gets portfolio from a drawer, and starts to put papers in it*)

STELLA MIDDLE-AGED
(*Rising*)

Very well. Perhaps it's for the best. I'll lay out pajamas for you, and a shirt or two. You'll be taking your overnight bag, will you, or d'you want something bigger?

MIDDLE-AGED

Don't do anything for me!

STELLA MIDDLE-AGED

As you wish. I think I'll go back to bed then, if you can spare me. I don't feel very well.

MIDDLE-AGED

I don't wonder.

STELLA MIDDLE-AGED

I haven't felt well all day.

MIDDLE-AGED

Something you ate.

STELLA MIDDLE-AGED

Perhaps. I don't know what it is. I keep getting these dizzy spells and having to sit down. There isn't an apple in the house, is there?

MIDDLE-AGED

Don't ask me. There may be in the kitchen. (*Suddenly looking at her*) I thought you hated apples.

STELLA MIDDLE-AGED

Normally I do, but suddenly I seem to want nothing else . . . (*She goes out.* MIDDLE-AGED *rises, looking after her. He entertains a doubt about her condition, dismisses it, then takes* MIRIAM's *photograph out of the drawer and is about to place it in the portfolio, when* YOUNG *emerges from the shadows*)

YOUNG

You swine!

(SAM *sits up*)

MIDDLE-AGED

What?

YOUNG

What have you done to her?

MIDDLE-AGED
(*Turning to face* YOUNG)
What the hell . . . ?

70

YOUNG

She's old and ugly.

MIDDLE-AGED

Well, you don't look all that beautiful any more, do you? Look at me!

(YOUNG *suddenly lunges at* MIDDLE-AGED. *They struggle and* MIRIAM's *photograph falls to the floor*)

SAM

Stop it!

MIDDLE-AGED

You young idiot! That's Miriam's photograph.

(*He picks up the photograph, puts it in the portfolio and goes to the door*)

SAM

See you in the morning.

MIDDLE-AGED

D'you really think so?

(*Smiling defiantly,* MIDDLE-AGED *goes.* YOUNG *is crestfallen, and wanders unhappily around.* SAM *watches him for a moment*)

SAM

What are you so depressed about?

YOUNG

Will he really come back?

71

SAM

Yes. He's only a man — no match for Stella. Those clever last words of hers will start to rankle! Apple!

YOUNG

You make Stella sound like . . . like an enemy.

SAM

(*Embarrassed. After a pause*)
Yes, well . . . sit down . . .
(YOUNG *sits on the footstool by the bed*)
Let me look at you . . . do you know, we hardly know each other, you and I?

YOUNG

No . . . no, we don't. . . .

SAM

Why are you so nervous? Does it worry you to look into your own old eyes, and see so much there you don't yet understand?

YOUNG

Not really, no. It seems a bit unreal.

SAM

We're different people, you know, you and I, but with the same name. You don't yet know what it's like to be me, and I can't really remember what it was like to be you. (*Chuckles gently. Pause*) Speak to me.

72

YOUNG

I don't really know what to say.

SAM

So shy . . . and so hopeful. (*He smiles*) You know, I think
we'll get on better with each other, than we got on with those
other two.

YOUNG

Oh?

SAM

Yes, because we're closer to the great mysteries of birth and
death than they are. They're somewhere near the height of
their powers, when a man struggles with all the problems of
maturity, and has no time and too much strength to care about
simplicity. D'you know what I mean?

YOUNG

Not really, no.

SAM

When you're very old, you know that a child has the right idea.
If only it had the authority. That's why I cherish you more than I
do . . . (*With a look round*) those other two, because our vision
is the same, except that yours is fresh, whereas mine is tinged
with vague imprecise memories of the long road I have traveled.
It's quite logical, when you come to think of it. After all dawn
and twilight tint the sky with much the same color — one is a
greeting, the other a valediction — but if you steal a glance at the

73

sky, you'd be hard put to it to know which is which. Naturally it doesn't do to sit and stare.

YOUNG

It seems to me though . . .

SAM

Yes, tell me, I'm eager to learn.

YOUNG

Don't think me impertinent.

SAM

No, no . . .

YOUNG

It seems to me that you make the same mistake as most of the old men I've met . . . my late headmaster, Daddy even . . . in that you treat the young as younger than they really are.

SAM

Oh well . . . that may be a little revenge perhaps . . . because you make us feel older than we really are.

YOUNG

I'm not a child.

SAM
(*With a sigh*)

No, no you're not. You're already halfway into the long tunnel . . . you keep glancing at the door.

74

YOUNG

Stella's up there with Mummy. . . . I'm waiting to see Daddy.

SAM

(*Alarmed*)

Not in here?

YOUNG

Yes, he doesn't like anyone in his study, but I'm sure he'll make an exception of today.

SAM

He'll have a heart attack if he finds me here. Can't you talk to him somewhere else?

YOUNG

No. No, I can't. It's a kind of declaration of independence. That's the way I see it anyway . . . the very fact of being here. After all, his only son doesn't get engaged every day.

SAM

Engaged? Today? Oh heavens!
(*He clutches his forehead*)

YOUNG

What is it?

SAM

After it's all over . . . the interview, I mean . . . don't come back in here to fetch Stella's coat.

75

YOUNG

Why should I?

SAM

She leaves it here.

YOUNG

Stella does?

SAM

Yes, don't come back to fetch it. Let her go home without it, if necessary.

YOUNG

But I can't. It's November. And what can I say to her if she says she left her coat in here. (*Rising*) That I haven't the nerve to fetch it?

SAM

No, no, you can't. Now Sam. This is frightfully important — whatever you do, make absolutely sure that she takes it with her when she leaves.

YOUNG

Why?

SAM

Because . . . Oh Sam, I haven't time to explain. Look, it's growing so much lighter.

(*It grows perceptibly lighter outside. The door opens, and a fairly attractive, plumpish* GIRL *in the costume of the late*

76

Victorian era enters. She closes the door. SAM *hides under his bedclothes. The* GIRL *goes to the desk, takes a key out of her pocket, and opens the same drawer as the one in which the photograph and the jewels were hidden. She takes out a letter, opens it and starts to read it. She smiles. Her expression changes according to the words she reads. It obviously means something very personal to her.* YOUNG *moves suddenly. The* GIRL *starts. Her name is* ADA COONEY. *She should be played by the actress who plays* CLARICE)

ADA

Oh, Master Sam, what are you doing here? Does Mr. Kinsale know you're here?

YOUNG

I don't know and I don't really care.

ADA
(After a momentary hesitation)
D'you want me to tell him? Or d'you want to sneak out?

YOUNG

I'm certainly not going to sneak out, no.

ADA
(After another hesitation)
I'll go and tell him then, shall I?

77

YOUNG

Why not? I'm in no hurry.

(ADA *puts the letter in her corsage and moves towards the door*)

ADA

Oh!

(*With a look at* YOUNG, *she goes out.* YOUNG *crosses to the desk.* SAM *stares at him*)

YOUNG

What does he keep in here?

SAM

In there he keeps . . . (*Frightened*) I don't remember.

(*As his father's voice is heard offstage,* SAM *hides under the covers again.* YOUNG *waits downstage.* REGINALD KINSALE, *the father of all the* SAMS, *enters, a florid Victorian gentleman with the kind of full mustache which gave the men of that period a pouting, cock o' the walk look. His whiskers brush back along the side of his face. He is of medium height, sure of himself, conservative and intolerant*)

REGINALD

(*Coming in, to the desk*)

What the dickens are you doing in here? You know perfectly well I don't like anyone in my study when I'm not here myself. Stand still, can't you? Swaying from one foot to the other like that. No need to be fidgety with me. Now, out with it.

YOUNG

Out with what, Dad?

78

REGINALD

Have you taken leave of your senses, young man? Not only are
you out of bounds, but Miss Cooney tells me you were insuffer-
ably arrogant — I believe you told her that you didn't care if I
knew of your presence here or not. Any truth in that?

YOUNG

I did say something of the sort, yes.

REGINALD

Eh?

YOUNG

Well, I think it is degrading for me not to be able to see you
when I want to — but to have to go through a servant.

REGINALD

Miss Cooney is my secretary. She is not a servant. And when
I was your age, I used to call my father "sir."

YOUNG

Is that what you want?

REGINALD

No, no, but it would have been nice if you'd thought of the
little courtesy by yourself . . . it's not something I'd ever dream
of asking for . . . I am aware that times have changed . . . we
live in a modern age, manners don't count any more.

YOUNG

It occurs to me, sir.

REGINALD

Yes?

YOUNG

It occurs to me that while you're surprised to see me in here, you're not at all eager to know *why* I'm here.

REGINALD

Do you think I can't guess?

YOUNG

Well, I wouldn't choose to come into your study, sir, unless I had some reason.

REGINALD

You need some money, do you? You're in some scrape.

YOUNG

Not that I know of, sir.

REGINALD

Eh? Well, what other reason . . . ? (*Suddenly alarmed*) You haven't made a fool of yourself, I mean . . . em . . . there's no girl involved, I trust . . . ?

YOUNG

Yes, there is.

REGINALD

Good God, man, aren't you ashamed of yourself? No! I don't

80

even want to know how it happened. One would have thought, wouldn't one, after the education I had given you — but there you are! Even with all the expense of one of our oldest public schools, my old school in fact . . . it makes no difference, does it? A moment of folly, and all restraint, all breeding, all honor is conveniently forgotten. You ought to be ashamed of yourself.

YOUNG

Why? Weren't you ever engaged to Mummy?

REGINALD

Eh? Is that all you are, engaged?

YOUNG

Yes.

REGINALD

There's no ugly little surprise on its way in . . . how shall I put it? . . . in nine months' time?

YOUNG

No.

REGINALD

You're quite sure?

YOUNG

Of course.

81

REGINALD

Hm. . . . (*He suddenly stops dead*) Engaged? You can't be. You're under age.

YOUNG

That's what I came to see you about.

REGINALD
(*Sitting at desk*)
No, no, it's out of the question. A boy of twenty's a mere child.

YOUNG

I only came as a courtesy, father. I'll be twenty-one in six weeks' time. We can wait that long — if necessary. Shall I go now, father?

REGINALD
(*With sudden affection*)
Now, Sam . . . (*Rises, reaching for a box of cigars on his desk*) I've always hoped for a real father and son relationship with you . . . a friendship, born of respect in you and pride in me . . . for some reason, that's not been possible. . . . (*Sighs, and clips his cigar*) Still, although your feeling for me is perhaps not what it should be, I do hope you will at least be prepared to listen to my counsel. And . . . em . . . there is no need to tell your mother the precise contents of our conversation. We're as man to man in here, in this august room, which one day will be yours. . . . (*He lights his cigar*) . . . I may have been a little annoyed to find you in here, but now, on mature reflection, I welcome your intrusion. . . . Yes, I'm glad you're here. . . . Cigar?

82

YOUNG

No thank you, sir.

REGINALD
(*Laughing heartily*)
I remember my first . . . my father gave it me . . . I was sick
as a dog. . . .
(YOUNG *joins in the laughter*)
vomited all over the floor . . . he took it in good part though
. . . I can hear him laughing to this day. Go on, have one.

YOUNG

No thank you, sir.

REGINALD

Why not?

YOUNG

I have no desire to vomit all over the floor.
(REGINALD *frowns. Truly, father and son have little in
common, he reflects, not without bitterness*)

REGINALD
(*Moving to sit at the desk*)
Now, what I'm going to tell you is perhaps what I should have
told you some time ago. We always think of our children as
youngsters, and then almost imperceptibly, they grow as tall as
we, and one day, the day we least expect, they're ready to go out
into the world. Yes. (*He sighs and draws on his cigar*) Don't
think of marriage until you're thirty, thirty-five even. . . .

83

YOUNG

What? Why not?

REGINALD

It's not fair to you, and it's not fair to the young lady.

YOUNG

Why not?

REGINALD
(*Rising*)

You ought to go out and acquire some experience . . . sow your wild oats, as they used to say.

YOUNG

A moment ago, you jumped to the conclusion that I had sown a wild oat, and you were most upset.

REGINALD

Yes, well, there's . . . there's no need to sow it without taking . . . elementary precautions.

YOUNG

What elementary precautions?

REGINALD

Good Lord, boy, did they teach you nothing at school? (*Sits again*) Well . . . I can't go into all that now. Sit down.
(YOUNG *sits at the other side of the desk*)
And if you don't know much about it, it's advisable to go to

Africa, or somewhere off the beaten track . . . so that there are no . . . as it were . . . embarrassing repercussions. . . .

YOUNG

I don't understand, I'm afraid. Maybe I'm simple-minded.

REGINALD

I consider that a fairly safe assumption.

YOUNG

But . . . what you're saying is the very opposite of what it says in the Bible.

REGINALD
(Rising, suddenly terrible)

Now look here! . . .

(YOUNG rises too)

I will not allow the Holy Writ to be intruded into this conversation. I have never, and will never tolerate blasphemy in my house. Is that clear? This is a practical and a profane conversation between two grown men, or at least, one and a half grown men, and it's in the very worst possible taste to bring the Bible into it. . . . (*He sits again,* YOUNG *follows suit*) At all events, Our Lord was a bachelor, and it's safe to assume that his instructions were theoretical rather than practical in these matters . . . the fact is, whether we like it or not, that an active male is not fit to settle down before the beginning of middle age . . . at least that gives the old demon his head for the most emotionally unstable years . . . and it does teach a fellow the technique of giving pleasure, without which, there's no pleasure to be had. . . .

85

YOUNG

But you didn't wait that long . . . you got married when you were twenty-two or twenty-three.

REGINALD

Twenty-three. That is precisely why I'm giving you this advice.

YOUNG
(*Horrified*)

Oh.

REGINALD

Yes. Now I want you to forget our little conversation, and forget all about getting engaged.

YOUNG

I can't. She's waiting.

REGINALD

Who?

YOUNG

Stella. She's upstairs with Mummy.

REGINALD

Stella? Is that the object of your affections? Hm. I don't trust your mother not to hold out hope for the young lady. She's so appallingly sentimental. I'll have to be rather stern, I'm afraid. What's her name again?

86

YOUNG

Stella.

REGINALD

Yes, yes, I heard that part of it.

YOUNG

Oh, Stella Chough.

REGINALD
(*Laughs*)
As in locomotive? Chuff-chuff . . . chuff-chuff?

YOUNG

Yes, I suppose so.

REGINALD
It's rather an abrupt name, isn't it?
(*The door opens, and* MRS. KINSALE, *a large lady with a
full bosom, sails into the room, accompanied by* STELLA)

MRS. KINSALE
Here we are, Reginald. Has Sam made his little speech?

REGINALD
Yes. Yes, he has indeed. Quite took me by surprise. How d'you
do, young lady. Sit down. Sit down.

MRS. KINSALE
I was quite frank, Reginald. I warned Stella that you'd prob-

ably be opposed to any precipitate action — that you'd be in favor of a long engagement at least.

REGINALD

Yes, yes, quite. Quite.

MRS. KINSALE

At the same time, they do seem very much in love.

REGINALD
(*Absently*)

Oh? . . . Oh? Curious we didn't know about it earlier.

MRS. KINSALE

Well, I've got a rather naughty secret . . . I did know.

REGINALD
(*Chuckles, humorlessly*)

Oh . . . kept it from Father, eh?

STELLA
(*Giggles*)

Yes. . . .

MRS. KINSALE
(*Coyly*)

Yes. . . .
(*A long and most embarrassing pause*)

REGINALD

Yes . . . well . . . your name is Chough, as I understand it.

SAM: They look like the feet of a twelfth-century monk
in a cathedral, don't they?
(*Act I, page 18*)

SAM: She's what the critics might call a nagger's nagger!
(*Act III, page 146*)

SAM: I'm not really allowed them, you know.
(*Act II, page 113*)

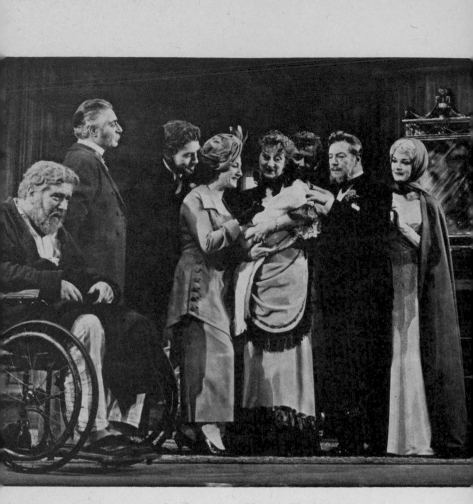

MR. KINSALE: He's got a sense of humor like his mother.
(*Act III, page 174*)

                    STELLA
Yes. (*Spelling it out*) C-h-o-u-g-h.

                    REGINALD
Oh, I see, not C-h-u-f-f.

                    STELLA
        (*With a blush and self-conscious giggle*)
Oh, Lord no. . . .
                    (*Pause*)

                    REGINALD
No . . . (*Absently puffing*) No . . . no . . . may one ask
what your father . . . em . . .

                    MRS. KINSALE
He's an officer, Reggie.

                    REGINALD
Now Agnes, I'm sure Miss Chough is quite capable of —

                    MRS. KINSALE
It's only that I'd already asked her —
                    (*These two lines tail off*)

                    STELLA
He's a major.

                    MRS. KINSALE
                    (*Echoing*)
A major.

REGINALD

Really? Yes . . . that's a good rank . . . a good intermediary
rank . . . between a captain and a colonel.

STELLA

Between a captain and a lieutenant colonel.

REGINALD
(*Vaguely irritated*)
Yes, well . . . we always like to give a lieutenant colonel the
benefit of the doubt, don't we, and we refer to him as a colonel.

STELLA

I think you'll find you're wrong. Daddy told me that on formal
invitations —

REGINALD
(*Angered*)
Where is he stationed?

STELLA

Daddy? He's in Africa.

REGINALD

Oh? Will he be there for long?

STELLA

He'll come home on leave in August.

MRS. KINSALE

Now, Reggie, wouldn't it be nice if —

90

REGINALD

(*Brushing her aside*)

Well, you know, I really feel it is essential for the two fathers to meet before we take any irrevocable step.

STELLA

Oh no. That's an awfully long time to wait.

REGINALD

Now Stella, you are under age, so is Samuel. It is the duty of Major Chough and of myself to protect you from yourselves until you are quite sure you know your own minds. I presume your mother . . . ?

MRS. KINSALE

Reggie!

STELLA

Mummy's dead.

REGINALD

Is she? Is she? And when did this deplorable . . . ?

STELLA

When I was born.

REGINALD

Oh, quite recently . . . how tragic . . . but then are you? . . . I mean does nobody . . . in your father's absence . . . ?

91

STELLA

I live with Granny . . . Lady Chough.

REGINALD
(*Expressing interest*)

Lady Chough?
(*He reaches slowly for the copy of* Who's Who *on the desk*)

MRS. KINSALE

She's a most remarkable old lady. I have had occasion to admire her needlework . . . the loveliest petit-point samplers and tea-cozies.

REGINALD
(*Looking her up in* Who's Who)

I see. You have taken tea with her? I surmise that negotiations have been in progress for some time before I was consulted.

MRS. KINSALE
(*Embarrassed*)

Lady Chough breeds pomeranians.

REGINALD

Pomeranians?

STELLA

Dogs . . .

YOUNG

She's promised us one as a wedding present.

REGINALD

I can imagine few more useful gifts to a young couple. Chough . . .

(*He begins to read. The other three express worry. Of what he reads, a few items raise his hopes; but foreboding is heavier in the balance*)

Your grandmother is a peeress in her own right, I see, marrying Esme Chough, Auctioneer! That is, or was, your grandfather, I presume.

STELLA

Was . . .

REGINALD

I'm sorry.

STELLA

Granny ran away from home to marry Grandpa. Her family didn't approve. They were wonderfully happy together right up to the end.

REGINALD

There are exceptions to every rule, of course. Auctioneer. Hm. (*Closes* Who's Who) Marriage is a very vital step, Stella. I like to think of it as a merger between two individuals. Now in the world of commerce, we do not arrange mergers just because we like members of a rival board, no, they are concluded because there is an advantage in a merger which is denied the two companies as independent entities. Please don't cry, Stella. Now the same rules, I submit, apply to the situation with which you have confronted me. You are aware, I am sure, that Samuel as my only

93

son, stands to inherit considerable wealth and a social position which I can, in all modesty describe as enviable . . .

YOUNG
(*Hotly*)

Dad! Can't you see that you're upsetting Stella?

STELLA

Sam, don't.

REGINALD

You wish me to be silent? Is that what I am to understand?

MRS. KINSALE

Now Reg, dear . . .

REGINALD

What?

MRS. KINSALE

Ils sont tellement jeunes.

REGINALD

Why on earth —

MRS. KINSALE

Je parle en français parce que je ne veux pas qu'ils comprenent ce que je dis.

REGINALD

I beg your pardon?

MRS. KINSALE

Ils sont amoureux. Remember what it was like?

REGINALD

What, pray?

MRS. KINSALE

To be in love.

REGINALD

Love never excused bad manners.

MRS. KINSALE

It is blind, if we are to believe the poet.

REGINALD

The poet never suggested, however, that it was either deaf or dumb. My father raised Cain when you turned out to be the daughter of a colonial bishop, remember? All the family needs now is the granddaughter of an auctioneer, and a small dog!

STELLA
(*Rising. Shaking with rage*)

Sam, I'd like to go, please.

MRS. KINSALE

Come upstairs, Stella. You haven't really finished your tea, you know — there's still a mille-feuille and an éclair left.

95

YOUNG
(*Livid*)
I'd just like to say one thing.

MRS. KINSALE
(*Emotionally maternal*)
No, Sam! Don't, my darling.

REGINALD
Why not, Agnes? His voice broke a few months ago. Let him get used to manhood. After all, il est amoureux.
(*After a moment of hesitation,* YOUNG *rushes from the room to prevent his tears from being visible.* STELLA *runs after him*)

STELLA
Sam! It doesn't make any difference.

MRS. KINSALE
I hope you're satisfied . . .

REGINALD
What are you complaining about? You heard her saying it makes no difference.

MRS. KINSALE
They're very young.

REGINALD
Precisely. It is the knowledge of that fact which has governed my every action this afternoon. There is nothing gratuitous about

96

my attitude, Agnes. Everything I do, I do for a purpose. This marriage, if allowed to take place, would end in disaster.

MRS. KINSALE

How can you be so sure?

REGINALD

Never mind. I know. A marriage can be ruined at the outset if the early intimacies are . . . how shall I phrase it? . . . if the wedding night is one long blush. They haven't even truly experienced physical desire. Oh, they dance together, hold hands in doorways, find it impossible to say goodnight, but that doesn't mean anything — that's just a projection of the puppy-love they had for their prefects at school.

MRS. KINSALE

Is that all our courtship meant to you?

REGINALD

I'm talking about them, not about us.

MRS. KINSALE

You're talking about us. You're trying to hurt me, through them.

REGINALD

You're the most self-centered person I've ever known.

MRS. KINSALE

And you're the cruelest.
      (*Smiling doggedly, she goes.* REGINALD *looks darkly at the*

97

floor for a moment, then takes a key from his pocket and opens the desk drawer. He finds it empty, and sighs. Then he rings the bell, and waits. As he waits, he passes his hand over his hair, straightens his tie. MISS COONEY *enters with some documents for his perusal*)

REGINALD

Ah, Miss Cooney.

ADA

Ah, Mr. Kinsale.

REGINALD

The return of sanity to the study . . . did you hear any of that?

ADA

I never listen at doors.

REGINALD

I am sure you saw Miss Chough, however. I would credit you with at least that amount of feminine curiosity.

ADA

I caught a fleeting glimpse of her, yes.

REGINALD

Fleeting enough to size up the thickness of her ankles, the shortness of her legs, the adolescent flush of her complexion.

98

ADA
(*Smiling*)

Fleeting, yes.

REGINALD

Mm . . . what d'you make of her?

ADA

She's well-spoken.

REGINALD

Did you hear her speak?

ADA

No, but she's got the shape of a girl who spends a lot of time on a horse. Horses cost money.

REGINALD

Broad in the beam.

ADA

No. She leans forward as she walks. Looks as though she's just about to jump a fence.

REGINALD
(*Laughing*)

My God, you're intelligent. I'd never have thought of that.

ADA

I couldn't run a coal mine. D'you want to work?

99

REGINALD

You got my letter.

ADA

Yes.

REGINALD

I opened the drawer to look for the answer.

ADA

Give me a chance.

REGINALD

I know. No, I don't want to work. I never really want to work when you're here.

ADA

Perhaps I ought to give notice.

REGINALD

Why d'you say that?

ADA

I'm thinking of the coal mine.

REGINALD

Hang the coal mine.

ADA

May I quote that?

100

REGINALD

To whom?

ADA

The Board.

REGINALD

I believe you might.

ADA
(*Arranging some papers*)

Oh?

REGINALD

There's an element of danger about you which I find irresistible.

ADA

You think I'm a femme fatale.

REGINALD
(*Flinching slightly*)

Stick to English, there's a sport. There's quite enough bad French around the house. (*Leaning towards her*) You've got spirit, Ada.

ADA

Spirit?

REGINALD
(*His nose in her ear now*)

And a glorious body.

101

ADA
(*Very casual*)

You'll make me blush.

REGINALD

Look at me.

ADA

I'm filing the correspondence with the Amalgamated Cast Iron Boiler Company.

REGINALD

Why?

ADA

If I don't, who will?

REGINALD

When may I expect an answer to my invitation?

ADA

I don't know. I'm not a very good correspondent.

REGINALD

You're too good to be a secretary.

ADA

Too good a what?

102

REGINALD

Naughty! You're teasing me. I don't mind. I can take it. One day you'll get married to some man your own age — then you'll make his life a misery as they all do — but until then, I want you . . . for my own.

ADA
(*Calm*)
Aren't you a little ashamed of yourself?

REGINALD

Not in the least, because you're practical. You've the mind of a man with all the other attributes of your own sex. It's an ideal combination. You're not sentimental. Some might even call you a little hard. I like that.

ADA
(*Holding up a paper from the desk*)
What are we going to do about the contract with the Dutch?

REGINALD
(*Taking it from her*)
We're going to file it and forget it. Ada, I'm getting a little annoyed with you.

ADA

Oh, dear.

REGINALD
(*Seizing her wrist*)
Come away from that desk.

ADA
Let me have my wrist back first, and then we'll see.

REGINALD
(*Lets go her wrist*)
Well?

ADA
(*Turning away*)
I didn't say I would.

REGINALD
(*Strident*)
Ada, I'm hopelessly in love with you. (*Pause*) I want you.
   (*Pause. She goes on arranging documents. He suddenly
seizes her. There is a struggle*)

ADA
I'll scream.

REGINALD
So will I!
   (*He forces her back onto the desk, drowning her cry with
the pressure of his kiss. She quickly becomes more passion-
ate than he.* YOUNG *enters, closes the door*)
         (*Lifting his head, seeing his son, outraged*)
104

Did no one ever tell you it was polite to knock before you enter a room?

YOUNG

Stella left her coat.
(*He takes it.* ADA *struggles free, and runs out of the room*)
I understand now what you mean about sowing your wild oats. Sir.
(REGINALD *strikes his son across the face.* SAM *sits up in bed, nursing his cheek*)

SAM

That's too much. I had almost forgotten that. Sam, help me out of bed.

REGINALD
(Recoiling in horror)

Who are you?

SAM

Me? I'm your son.

REGINALD
(Quaking)

Samuel . . . you knew about this man's presence in here?

YOUNG
(Helping SAM up)

Of course . . . it's me.

105

REGINALD

What d'you mean?

YOUNG

It's me . . . what I will be like.

REGINALD
(*A melodramatic whisper*)

A ghost!

(*He backs away*)

SAM
(*Advancing slowly on* REGINALD)

A ghost! You fathead. What a charming Victorian over-simplification. A ghost! I'm your son. If anyone's a ghost, *you* are.

REGINALD
(*Heaving slightly*)

How dare you suggest that I'm a ghost?

SAM

I never suggested any such thing. I don't believe in them in any case. And I have every reason to believe in you, sir. I can feel that blow as though it were yesterday.

YOUNG

Actually it's today.

106

SAM

So it is, Sam, so it is. The day you first misguidedly brought Stella to see the old man.

REGINALD

You agree with me then, whoever you are?

SAM

I agree with you, you idiot, of course I do, even to the point of being unreasonable. Don't you understand that it was you and no one else who drove me into Stella's arms at the age of twenty-one?

REGINALD

You mean you disobeyed me?

SAM

Of course I did. Who with an ounce of guts in him would have obeyed you?

REGINALD

Then the blame is yours, not mine!

SAM

You gave me no choice!

REGINALD

I gave you every choice!

SAM

That might have been true until the moment I found you trying

107

to rape Miss Ada Cooney on that desk, when I saw you as the filthy hypocrite you are . . . your formal suiting living one life, and the naked man beneath, another.

REGINALD

If you are, as you say, my son, I forbid you to talk to me like that.

SAM

You have no right to forbid me anything. You may be my father but I'm older than you are! In fact, I'm older than you ever will be . . . you don't live to be my age. You die!

YOUNG

Sam, don't go on talking. It won't do any good.

SAM

Leave me alone! I never thought I'd have the opportunity. You die . . . under the most embarrassing circumstances.

REGINALD
(*Staggering back to the desk*)
What d'you mean?

SAM
(*Eager to whisper into his father's ear*)
Shall I tell you?

REGINALD
(*He stops up his ears*)
I don't want to know! (*His curiosity slowly overcomes him*)
D'you mean, I die in the arms of . . . of Ada Cooney?

108

SAM

Oh, no. Ada Cooney gave notice the next morning. We'd seen too much of the way you conducted your affairs. From now on you have to take your pleasures where you can. You don't even know the young lady's name.

REGINALD
(*Sits at desk*)

Oh, God!

SAM

Oh, God! What are you thinking of now?

REGINALD

The scandal.

SAM

The scandal . . . but you weren't here to face the music, were you . . .

REGINALD
(*Pathetic*)

I was always so careful . . .

SAM

Yes careful, weren't you! (*Volcanic*) On this desk you were careful!

YOUNG

Did it help to do that?

109

SAM
(*A roar*)

What?

YOUNG

Did it help to do that?

SAM
(*Pausing, then slowly*)

No. It was unforgivable. (*Pause*) I'm sorry, Dad.

REGINALD

When does this occur?

SAM

Oh, you've got some little time yet.

REGINALD

That's not true, is it? Out with it.

SAM

About three or four weeks . . .

REGINALD
(*Dully*)

Three or four weeks . . .

SAM
(*To* YOUNG)

I only did that to protect you, you know.

110

YOUNG

I can look after myself.

SAM

What?

YOUNG

I'm strong. I'm in love. Cheer up, Dad.

REGINALD

I apologize, son.

YOUNG
(*Lightly*)

Oh, that's all right, sir. I understand.
(*He goes*)

SAM
(*Sad*)

He says he understands. He doesn't.

REGINALD

You do though, don't you?

SAM

In a way . . . I'm afraid . . . I do.

REGINALD

Am I really so different from other men?

111

SAM

How can I tell? I'm only another man. If I were any more than that, I'd have refrained from taking that stupid revenge on you just now.

REGINALD

Oh, I think I knew I hadn't much longer, old man. I seem to be in such a hurry. I can't . . . Why are you laughing?

SAM

It's funny, you calling me old man.

REGINALD

Yes, it is . . .

SAM
(*After a pause*)
I say, might I accept that cigar now, do you think?

REGINALD

What? Oh, yes . . . of course.

SAM

I'm afraid I can't guarantee to vomit all over the floor.

REGINALD
(*Producing his cigar-cutter*)
Would you like me to cut it for you?

112

SAM

I would be obliged, yes sir, if you can see your way to doing it.
(REGINALD *lights a match for his son*)
I'm not really allowed them, you know.

REGINALD

I'm not allowed them, either. Heart.

SAM

Hereditary.

REGINALD

Yes.

(REGINALD *relights his cigar*)

SAM

There's nothing like a good cigar to help you think.
(*Sits opposite* REGINALD)

REGINALD

Or not to think, as the case may be . . .

SAM

Yes!

(*He laughs*)

REGINALD

What did you do with your life, Sam?

SAM

Oh, nothing much. I wrote.

113

REGINALD

Oh? Did you persist in that just because I was opposed to it?

SAM

No. I thought I had some talent.

REGINALD

(*Incredulous*)

Really. Poetry.

SAM

Poetry to start with. Then I went on to rather obscure novels.

REGINALD

Mm. Didn't pay, I bet. You needed all your inheritance to live.

SAM

Not all of it, no. Later I went into more commercial stuff, with some detective stories and a few horrors.

REGINALD

Ah, that's more my cup of tea. There's nothing I like better than a good ration of horror. Ghost stories.

SAM

Ghosts! Then afterwards I found a style which was rather more artistic. People seemed to like it. All in all, I made quite a lot of money.

114

REGINALD

How extraordinary. Congratulations. And what happened to the coal mine?

SAM

They nationalized it.

REGINALD

Good grief! Nationalized? Are we still a monarchy?

SAM

Oh yes. I say, this is an awfully good cigar . . .

REGINALD

Yes, isn't it.

SAM

They don't make these like that any more.

REGINALD

I'm not a bit surprised. It's just as well I did die, you know. I'd have found it all too confusing.

SAM

Yes, I think you're better off.

REGINALD

You married Stella, did you?

SAM

Mm.

REGINALD

Divorced?

SAM

No.

REGINALD
(*Surprised*)

Really?

SAM

You never really liked Stella, did you?

REGINALD
(*Rising*)

No, quite frankly, I didn't. They blush very prettily when they're young, those girls, and have all the appearance of demureness — but they were brought up in a hard school, and they're just biding their time. Suddenly they strike. If there are no children, they become harsh and unpleasant as people can be . . . we can't really blame them, after all, we're not women, that's something we can never understand. But if there are children, they become possessive, and domestic life becomes a useless and heartbreaking battle. That's more difficult to come to terms with. Am I right?

SAM

How do you know all this?

116

REGINALD

Remember your Auntie Alice?

SAM

Who?

REGINALD

Auntie Alice, my sister? Absolute first-class bitch. She married an admiral, who later committed suicide instead of coming home on leave. Their son designs lampshades, if you understand me, and his mother rules him with a rod of iron to this day. I'll be quite frank with you, when you brought your Stella in here, it quite bowled me over. I said to myself, "Good God, it's Alice."

SAM

Alice? Why, did they look alike?

REGINALD

Spitting image.

SAM

No! How macabre for you! But tell me, do you really think it's all their fault?

REGINALD

Good Lord, no. But they think it's all our fault when they get together and smoke their cigars or whatever they do. It'd be un-natural for us not to grouse when we're together.

117

SAM

But apart from that, sir, you weren't faithful, were you?

REGINALD

No.

SAM

No. But I suppose Mummy, on the other hand . . . ?

REGINALD

Oh, I'm quite sure she was. But then she had her smile. I never knew her not to smile, as though she were carrying out some secret message on behalf of her Maker through a hostile world. It drove me absolutely mad.

SAM
(*Chuckling*)

That's Mummy all over.

REGINALD

Of course, your Stella had her secret fury. They're not without their compensations.
(*He laughs*)

SAM
(*Suddenly*)

Oh, you would have laughed to see her smiling at your funeral! I shouldn't laugh. (*His effort to control himself only makes it worse*) Don't men disgust you?

118

REGINALD

Frequently. Women disgust me more, however.

SAM

(*Laughing*)

What, all of them? . . . Oh no, sir . . . come along, we can't allow that!

REGINALD

No. (*Seriously*) There's one I frequently think of to this day. A woman I never had an affair with, never even met more than once, and that at a party with many other people there. I never even caught her name properly. I have no idea if she was married or single. We didn't even talk very much — just stood and stared at one another. It was extraordinary. Oh, I could have found out all about her from my host, but for some reason, I didn't want to do anything that might spoil that moment . . . perhaps the truest moment of my life, when words were unnecessary . . . there was just a curious . . . understanding, a sadness, a resignation, a glimpse of infinite depth and blinding light . . .

SAM

And you never even knew her name . . .

REGINALD

Oh, someone called her away from me, and I gathered that her first name was . . . Miriam.

SAM

(*Hushed*)

How extraordinary.

119

REGINALD

Why?

SAM
(*With a feeling of guilt in spite of himself*)
Well, it's not a very usual name, is it?

REGINALD

No, it isn't . . .
(*Pause*)

SAM

No. Miriam . . . It's more unusual than usual, I would say . . .
Funny . . . You know, you don't seem to be at all the same man
as the one I was so angry with just now. You don't even seem to
be the father I remember.

REGINALD

Is the father we remember ever the father as he saw himself?

SAM

I have no wish to appear presumptuous . . . you being . . .
who you are — if you understand me . . . Daddy . . . but it occurs to me that we would have got on awfully well if only we had
been contemporaries.

REGINALD

By Jove, that's true.
(*The door opens and* ELDERLY *staggers in, obviously in
considerable pain*)
Who's that?

120

SAM
(*Uninterested*)
That? That's me.

REGINALD
You? How long ago?

SAM
Oh, about twenty years.

REGINALD
(*Laughing*)
You seem to be in a bad way.
(ELDERLY *falls onto the bed*)

SAM
(*Sadly*)
Yes. Well, it's the old . . . (*He indicates his heart, then points to his father's*) As I said, it's hereditary.
(*As* REGINALD *continues to chuckle* . . .)

THE CURTAIN FALLS

121

Act Three

ACT THREE

The same room. SAM, *in his wheelchair, is writing at the desk, his glasses on his nose. He is smoking his cigar.* ELDERLY *is lying on the bed. He groans.* SAM *expresses irritation.* ELDERLY *groans again.*

SAM

I really can't concentrate on my work if you persist in making that repellent sound.

ELDERLY
(*Looking up with difficulty*)
Have you no pity?

SAM

You wish me to have self-pity? No. I've given it up as a waste of time.

ELDERLY

But I'm in pain.

SAM

You survive, though. I happen to know that.

125

ELDERLY

How can you be so brutal? Do you know what the doctor told me?

SAM

Of course I do. I was there.

ELDERLY

No women, no spirits, no smoking. What are you doing with that cigar?

SAM

Enjoying it.

ELDERLY

Don't you know they're forbidden?

SAM

I've come to terms with my illness. Dad gave it me.

ELDERLY

Who?

SAM

Dad. Our Daddy!

ELDERLY

Awful swine. When did . . . (*He has a momentary pain*) Oh . . . When did you see him?

126

SAM
(*Writing*)

Sssh!
(*He mouths the words he is writing. When* ELDERLY *talks he shakes his head with irritation as he attempts to maintain his concentration*)

ELDERLY
(*After a pause*)

What are you writing? (*He has some difficulty breathing*) What are you writing?

SAM

Oh!! (*Giving up*) You used to complain that Stella gave you no peace. You're worse than she is. What do you want to know?

ELDERLY

I asked you what you were writing.

SAM

Our autobiography.

ELDERLY

Steady now. You'd better not tell more than half the truth, what?

SAM

What do you mean by that?

ELDERLY

Well, look at me.

127

SAM

Sam, sometime near the end of life, there's a reckoning — not with God — with yourself. Maybe it's the same thing. . . . You begin to wonder who you are, what you are, what gifts you had, which you used, which you neglected, which you abused. (*He looks with amusement at his pages*) You asked me what I'm writing. I had written most of it already. Now I'm busy crossing things out. I made so many mistakes. I was writing it as one man. I'm thousands.

ELDERLY

What d'you mean?

SAM

I'm the two of us, the Sams we know, the Sams we don't and all the others in between. I sometimes look at myself in the mirror and hardly know what I see there — a portrait of eighty years with an infinity of other portraits just visible underneath.

ELDERLY

I never thought that writing would one day be so much trouble.

SAM

Oh, it's not writing that's the trouble, Sam, it's thought, and it's protecting thought against elegance, wit, style. . . . Oh, how I hate it.

ELDERLY

You hate it? Why? I would have thought —

128

SAM

Style's a way of lying. Style's an ornament which hides the architecture. (*He studies the manuscript*) A gorgeous turn of phrase that.

ELDERLY

Read it to me.

SAM
(*Scratching furiously*)
Too late. I've crossed it out.

ELDERLY

Why?

SAM

It was me at my worst.

ELDERLY

Wasn't it us, at our most typical. I thought you wanted to be honest in our confessions?

SAM
(*Sighing*)
You may be right at that. Confound you. You've some of my intelligence.

ELDERLY

What are you writing now?

129

SAM

I'm putting it back in again. (*Pause*) You know, Sam, I'd be the most honest of men, if only I was sure what honesty is.
(*The door opens, and* MIDDLE-AGED *appears. He is shaken*)

MIDDLE-AGED

She's pregnant!

SAM

I told you she would be.

MIDDLE-AGED

I don't know whether to laugh or to cry, or . . . she's her old self again . . . I've never seen her look so radiant . . . isn't it odd . . . (*Suddenly sees* ELDERLY, *and starts*) Oh, get up, you disgust me.

ELDERLY

I'm sick.

SAM

He's sick.

MIDDLE-AGED

D'you wonder . . . (*Abruptly gentle. His mood approaches hysteria, with its sudden changes*) A child . . . I wonder if it'll be a boy or a girl . . .

SAM

Tommy doesn't sound much like a girl, does it?

130

MIDDLE-AGED

Of course, a boy. Then the line is assured.

SAM

Yes, what there is of it.

MIDDLE-AGED

We're going to open a bottle of champagne. (*Suddenly remembers*) Oh . . .
    (MIDDLE-AGED *goes to the desk, opens it hastily and finds the photograph of* MIRIAM. STELLA's *voice is heard: "Sam!"*)

MIDDLE-AGED

Coming!

SAM

Hadn't you better add something a little more personal? Coming . . . ?

MIDDLE-AGED

Coming, sweetheart.
        (*He looks regretfully at the photo*)

SAM

That's better. (*As* MIDDLE-AGED *starts to tear up the photograph*)
        (*To* ELDERLY)
As for you, Sam, cover yourself up. Champagne, remember? (*Wheels himself hastily into the shadows*)
    (MIDDLE-AGED *finishes tearing up the photograph, and is just in time to stuff the remaining pieces into his pocket as*

131

STELLA MIDDLE-AGED *enters. She is dressed attractively and looks younger than we remember her*)

STELLA MIDDLE-AGED
(*Amused*)
Sam! What are you doing in here?

MIDDLE-AGED
Nothing . . . my love . . .

STELLA MIDDLE-AGED
Have you got the champagne?

MIDDLE-AGED
No, not yet.

STELLA MIDDLE-AGED
But I thought that's what you came down for.

MIDDLE-AGED
Yes, but you know me . . . I got sidetracked.

STELLA MIDDLE-AGED
(*Gently reproachful*)
Now darling, I've never been pregnant before. Surely your book can wait.

MIDDLE-AGED
Oh, heavens, yes. It wasn't the book. I thought I left something down here.

132

STELLA MIDDLE-AGED
What?

MIDDLE-AGED
(*With a trace of irritation*)
Please don't cross-examine me, Stella.

STELLA MIDDLE-AGED
Would you rather forget the champagne?

MIDDLE-AGED
Of course not. I'm sorry. I'll run and get it.

STELLA MIDDLE-AGED
You can walk if you like, Sam. After all, as a prospective father, you've got to be careful.

MIDDLE-AGED
(*With an awkward laugh*)
Yes. Why don't we go upstairs and drink it?

STELLA MIDDLE-AGED
No, I think it's a kind of poetic justice to drink it in here. I hate this room. It's caused me so much misery. I like to feel your father's spirit lingering around as we toast our embryo.

MIDDLE-AGED
Stella, this is supposed to be a happy occasion. I wouldn't like to think —

STELLA MIDDLE-AGED

(*Playfully insistent, her voice hushed*)

Get the champagne. I'm thirsty.

MIDDLE-AGED

I don't remember where it's kept.

STELLA MIDDLE-AGED

In the larder . . . you oaf!

(MIDDLE-AGED *goes.* STELLA *looks round the room, wanders over to the desk. She tries the drawers. They all slide open easily with the exception of one. She pulls at it, and appears puzzled. She looks around, sees the two or three bits of photograph on the floor. She kneels and picks them up. She tries to fit them together. They don't match, they are obviously pieces of something much larger. Her expression doesn't change at all. Carefully she puts the pieces back where she found them, spacing them at the correct intervals. After she has risen,* MIDDLE-AGED *comes back with a half-bottle of champagne and a couple of beer mugs*)

MIDDLE-AGED

(*Coming to the desk*)

All I could find in the way of glasses are a couple of beer mugs.

STELLA MIDDLE-AGED

What would happen if I died? You wouldn't know what to do, would you?

MIDDLE-AGED

If you'd only tell me where they are —

STELLA MIDDLE-AGED

It doesn't matter, it's symbolic of the Bohemian atmosphere you like to cultivate.

MIDDLE-AGED

Don't talk about dying, Stella.

STELLA MIDDLE-AGED

Why not. It'd solve so many problems . . . yours . . . mine . . . our child's.

MIDDLE-AGED

We're not going back to the old atmosphere again, are we? I was just saying it had changed . . . it was like it was at the very beginning.

STELLA MIDDLE-AGED

Oh? Whom did you say that to?

MIDDLE-AGED

What? I said it . . . to myself, naturally.

STELLA MIDDLE-AGED

And what was your reaction when you said that to yourself?

MIDDLE-AGED

What are you driving at?

STELLA MIDDLE-AGED

Am I being as obscure as your books? I'm sorry. I'm trying hard to find a language you'll understand.

135

MIDDLE-AGED

Stella, d'you want me to open this bottle, or don't you?

STELLA MIDDLE-AGED

Desperately.

MIDDLE-AGED

Then can we be pleasant?

STELLA MIDDLE-AGED

Yes, by all means. Let's be constructive.

MIDDLE-AGED

Not constructive. Pleasant.

STELLA MIDDLE-AGED

Oh Sam, open the champagne. I've got a tummy-ache. It must be all those apples I ate.
(MIDDLE-AGED *opens the bottle, and pours the champagne into the beer mugs*)
What d'you think it'll be?

MIDDLE-AGED

A boy.

STELLA MIDDLE-AGED

What if it's a girl?

MIDDLE-AGED

Then it's a girl. So long as it's something. (*Handing her a mug*)
Well, here's to the three of us.

136

STELLA MIDDLE-AGED
(*Rising*)
Perhaps it'll be four. Twins run in my family.

MIDDLE-AGED
The more the merrier.
(*They drink*)

STELLA MIDDLE-AGED
Delicious. Aren't you going to ask me to sit down?

MIDDLE-AGED
I don't like this room. Let's go upstairs.

STELLA MIDDLE-AGED
Why? I find this room most impressive. Of course, it suited a coal company better than it does a writer of advanced fiction.

MIDDLE-AGED
I hope we can move somewhere smaller, more intimate.

STELLA MIDDLE-AGED
Don't be silly, Sam. Thank God you've got the house. We couldn't afford to pay the rent of a decent place on the money you earn. Now, about schools.
(*Pause*)

MIDDLE-AGED
What?

137

STELLA MIDDLE-AGED

We must be practical. In case it's a boy, I have already written to the headmaster of your old school, and made an application to have him entered.

MIDDLE-AGED

But as you say yourself, what if it's a girl?

STELLA MIDDLE-AGED

Then her education won't matter, will it?

MIDDLE-AGED

Why not?

STELLA MIDDLE-AGED

All that matters for a girl is domestic science, to know where the champagne glasses are kept.

MIDDLE-AGED

Now, Stella! Really!

STELLA MIDDLE-AGED
(*Holding up a restraining hand*)

I'm fragile!

MIDDLE-AGED

Well, I've finished.

STELLA MIDDLE-AGED

Have some more.

138

MIDDLE-AGED

No.

STELLA MIDDLE-AGED

I will.

MIDDLE-AGED
(*Ignoring her*)
D'you mean to say that your first reaction on hearing that you were going to have a child was to sit down and write a letter to the headmaster of that uncouth and drafty academy where my will-power was broken?

STELLA MIDDLE-AGED

That was not my first reaction, no. My first reaction was to share my joy with the child's father, but he was nowhere to be found. He had left me, for good, remember?

MIDDLE-AGED
(*Contrite, refilling her glass*)
I'm sorry, darling. You knew I'd be back though, didn't you? I mean, I've never left you for very long.

STELLA MIDDLE-AGED

You sometimes leave the room. It was the first time you'd ever left the house.

MIDDLE-AGED

And the last time, Stella, I promise you.

139

STELLA MIDDLE-AGED

Well, that's nice to know.

MIDDLE-AGED

(*Dropping to his knees beside her*)

Let's fall in love again . . . it is possible . . . we both had such high hopes . . . they were identical, those hopes, and it's terribly important we should have them in common . . . Especially now since we have a new little person in which to invest those hopes . . .

STELLA MIDDLE-AGED

You're being wonderfully sentimental, Sam. If you only wrote the way you talked, you'd make a mint of money.

MIDDLE-AGED

I'm not going to rise to that. I'm being sincere. After all, Stella, however much pleasure a child may give us, he doesn't come into the world for that sole purpose. He's not here just for our benefit — he's got a life of his own to lead, and in order to get a good start, he needs a calm, harmonious family background, and that's up to us.

STELLA MIDDLE-AGED

You talk as though he were already ten years old, and I was being my usual possessive, and what's your word — calculating self.

MIDDLE-AGED

You've too long a memory, darling. We can never make a fresh start if you keep remembering.

140

STELLA MIDDLE-AGED

Teach me to forget then.

MIDDLE-AGED

(*After a pause*)

Will it help if I say I know my weaknesses. I am helpless, muddle-headed, childish in many ways — most irritating to live with — I have a hot temper — I'm awfully impractical, pretentious, and I often hate myself as much as you hate me.

STELLA MIDDLE-AGED

Is that all?

MIDDLE-AGED

What d'you mean?

STELLA MIDDLE-AGED

You make no mention of your roving eye, of the winning simper you put on in the presence of women.

MIDDLE-AGED

Now don't be greedy, Stella! I was doing very well in my confession. That doesn't mean anything, and you know it. If I have a certain natural charm, I can't really help it, can I? After all, what made you fall for me?

STELLA MIDDLE-AGED

I was awfully young. Your father was right.

MIDDLE-AGED

(*Hardens for a moment*)

Yes, he was.

141

STELLA MIDDLE-AGED

It's his victory, all this. (*Rises*) That's why I wanted to toast him, not us. He's come out of our marriage with flying colors.

MIDDLE-AGED
(*Rising*)
Don't you want to struggle? Is there no fight left in you?

STELLA MIDDLE-AGED

I'll need all my strength in the coming months. Afterwards we'll see . . .

MIDDLE-AGED

Come upstairs, Stella . . . This room has a bad influence on us.
(*She is crying silently. He
turns her round*)
You're crying!

STELLA MIDDLE-AGED

Not much . . .

MIDDLE-AGED

Then there is hope!
(*He tries to kiss her, she rejects him*)

STELLA MIDDLE-AGED
What about the bottle and the glasses?

MIDDLE-AGED
Oh, never mind the bottle and the glasses. The maid can clear them up in the morning. Darling . . . darling Stella.
(*This time he kisses her, and she responds. It begins as a
duty, ends as a lover's kiss*)

142

STELLA MIDDLE-AGED
(*Breaking from him*)

All right, let's go upstairs then . . . it doesn't matter about
the bottle, but I shouldn't leave your photography all over the
floor for everyone to see.

(*Before* MIDDLE-AGED *can think of a suitable reaction,*
STELLA *has left. He picks up the pieces of photograph, tries
to fit them together*)

MIDDLE-AGED
(*To himself*)

You can't tell anything from these bits . . .

SAM
(*Wheeling himself back into the light*)

It's not the bits that matters, it's the fact that you tore it up.

MIDDLE-AGED

Oh, are you still there? Did you watch?

SAM
(*With a sigh*)

I remember . . .

MIDDLE-AGED

What can I do?

143

SAM

You might choose another hiding place, to start with. The handle of this drawer must be covered with fingerprints and hardly any of them are yours.

MIDDLE-AGED

You mean she spies on me?

SAM

You know she does. You rather like it, in fact. It's your way of telling her there's a part of you she can never have. Women are possessive about things and other people. Men are possessive about themselves. Poor Stella!

MIDDLE-AGED

Are you taking her part now?

SAM

Yes.

MIDDLE-AGED

Why?

SAM

Because she's out of the room. If she were here, I'd back you up to the hilt.

MIDDLE-AGED

Tell me, did you ever give up hiding things in this drawer?

144

SAM

Since you ask, I go still further in sheer satanism. I still keep the drawer locked . . . but it's empty.

MIDDLE-AGED

Does that drive her mad?

SAM

Yes. We are creatures of habit, you know, Sam, and it so quickly becomes a habit to have bad manners. She's much more difficult to live with now than she was in your day. She's an old lady now and her beastliness has real sweep and majesty to it, superb control, especially on the back hand. It takes another nagger to appreciate the sheer beauty of it. She's what the critics might call a nagger's nagger!

MIDDLE-AGED

It's all very well for you to laugh about it.

SAM

What else d'you expect me to do? Weep? While you're dawdling down here, she's hard at work upstairs perfecting the techniques she'll one day use on me. Have you noticed, she hasn't even called you as she used to do? (*He imitates her*) Sam! Sam! Oh, what a weapon she's got with a child inside her. You won't be able to say a thing from now on. Every time you open your mouth to express an opinion she'll sit down or faint, and then she'll say, "Oh, if only you men knew the agony we go through, then perhaps you'd treat us as we deserve."

145

MIDDLE-AGED
(*Pale*)

What d'you want me to do?

SAM

Go up and talk to her, but try not to listen. It'll only upset you.

MIDDLE-AGED

You're upsetting me.

SAM

I'm sorry. But that little scene annoyed me so. I know perfectly well I may be entirely in the wrong, but I resent it bitterly. That's the trouble with people who live for revenge. They're never quite sure when they've had it — and so, to be on the safe side, they go on and on and on, endlessly. Don't fiddle with those bits of photography. Go up to her. And try to find some other hiding place. Do something positive!

(*Uncertainly,* MIDDLE-AGED *goes.* SAM *looks darkly at* ELDERLY, *who sits up laboriously*)

And that's the aegis under which young Tommy came into the world.

ELDERLY

How is he now?

SAM

Oh, much as he was at Angmering. A bachelor born. Wears a cloth cap and drives an open sports car, mainly in wet weather. Very close to Stella. Letters keep arriving, written in green ink.

146

She hoards them upstairs. . . . I never ask to see them. I'm not inquisitive. That's *my* revenge. Part of it.

ELDERLY

What does he do?

SAM

He works for the Government of South Australia, refusing immigrants. That might seem a slightly negative career to us, but I suppose it's an adequate reaction against his father and the wild world of the arts.

ELDERLY

If he refuses immigrants, he probably accepts them as well.

SAM

No, they've got another man to do that.

ELDERLY

Has he a flat?

SAM

I suppose he must have. Otherwise he'd be here, wouldn't he?
    (ELDERLY *rises with difficulty, taking* SAM's *stick*)
Where are you going with my stick?

ELDERLY

Surely you don't begrudge me your stick, do you?

SAM

Well, you might ask.

147

ELDERLY

(*Moving slowly towards the door*)
You're getting senile.

SAM

That's very rude. You haven't told me yet where you're taking
it.

ELDERLY

Into the garden. I've got so much explaining to do — I've got
to think it out. Incidentally, just for the record . . .
(*Tapping the wheelchair with the stick*)

SAM

Oh, don't do that!

ELDERLY

. . . how much money will you leave when you die?

SAM

Money, it's always money, with you, isn't it? About fifty thousand pounds.

ELDERLY

Hm. Not bad.

SAM

And if you hadn't bought Clarice that necklace it would have
been fifty-seven thousand pounds.
(ELDERLY *goes out*)
(SAM *begins to write again, when the door bursts open*

148

and a MAN *in his late thirties bursts in. He has a red mus-tache, and carries a flat cap and woolly scarf. It is* TOMMY.
He can be played by the actor playing YOUNG)

TOMMY

Dad?

SAM

Oh! Who's that? You gave me the most awful shock, Tommy!

TOMMY

Saw the light under your door —

SAM

Did no one ever tell you it's polite to knock before you enter?
What are you doing here at this time of night?

TOMMY

It's only two-thirty.

SAM

Why have you got that fatuous grin on your face? Are you in
trouble of some sort?

TOMMY

No.

SAM

You are, aren't you? You've driven your car into a tree. Killed
it?

149

TOMMY

No. I'll give you one more guess.

SAM

Will you? They've asked you to be Prime Minister of South Australia.

TOMMY

No. I'm going to be married.

SAM

No!

TOMMY

Yes.

SAM

I don't believe you.

TOMMY

Any objection?

SAM

Is she colored?

TOMMY
(*Shocked*)

Good Lord, no.

150

SAM

Great pity, if you don't mind my saying so. The family could do with a little new blood, you know. Not yellow at all? Not one of those interesting ladies, always on their knees?

TOMMY
(*Offended*)
Dad, I don't know how to take what you're saying.

SAM

Without ill-feeling, Tommy, for heaven's sake! It's just my way of telling you that I'm delighted: delighted. (*Irritated*) I don't care who she is.
(*He returns briefly to his work*)

TOMMY
Well, I do.

SAM
Well, it's your prerogative.

TOMMY
D'you want to meet her?

SAM
Do let me finish this sentence, will you? Do I want what? Do I want to meet her? Yes, if you have no objection.

TOMMY
I told her to beware of you.

151

SAM

Why did you do that?

TOMMY

She's read your books, anyway. She knows roughly what to expect.

SAM

Thomas, I don't know whether it's because we see each other so rarely, but there seems to be something rather aggressive in your attitude. I don't like it.

TOMMY

I'm not aggressive, Dad. I just don't see why . . . I came in here with some news I personally thought would — well, excite you — and in a matter of moments the whole thing seems to go rancid.

SAM

Rancid . . . that's a word I used very often in my younger days. I overworked it, I think. But it's a strong word, an unexpected word. Now, where were we? Oh yes, you were telling me about some yellow lady in a tree. (*A sudden flash of memory*) Oh, no! Congratulations! Now, there's a little ritual in our family on these occasions — (*Pulls over the cigar box, opens it*) Oh, I'm afraid there aren't any left.

TOMMY

I thought you weren't allowed them anyway.

152

SAM

Well, sit down. We might thrash this thing out.

TOMMY

I can't now. She's waiting.

SAM

Who's that?

TOMMY
(*Fed up*)

My fiancée.

SAM

Where?

TOMMY

Outside.

SAM

Bring her in!

TOMMY

Are you sure you don't mind?

SAM

Oh Tommy! — I was joking!

TOMMY
(*Opening the door, calling*)

Alice!

SAM

(*Softly. With foreboding*)

Alice?

(*A* GIRL *enters who resembles* STELLA *at the age of twenty most strikingly*)

ALICE

(*Who speaks with the appalling languor of the English upper classes, although she is dressed in trousers and a duffel-coat*)

I'm terribly sorry we're so late, Mr. Kinsale.

TOMMY

Dad . . . this is Alice . . . Alice Montego.

SAM

Montego. Well, there we are. Excuse my not rising, my dear . . . I'm afraid I'm a bit of an old crock.

ALICE

That's all right, please don't bother. As I was saying, I didn't want to come here tonight at all, you know. (*Suddenly very loud, as though Sam were deaf*) I didn't want to risk waking you up . . . but Tommy insisted.

SAM

Tommy, aren't you going to ask this thing to sit down somewhere over there?

(*He indicates a distant part of the room*)

154

ALICE
(*Sitting down near Sam*)
It's all right, Tommy, I can manage.

TOMMY
Champagne! The very thing! Just what the doctor ordered.
(*He tries the remains of a glass, pulls a face*) Oh! It's flat and
sour.

SAM
(*Amused*)
I'm not surprised. It's been there for some time.

TOMMY
At all events, you can't complain. Champagne and cigars.

SAM
(*Quietly*)
I'm not complaining, Tom.

ALICE
I must say, I adore your writing.

SAM
Oh . . . (*Nods, flattered. To* TOMMY) D'you hear that?

ALICE
I remember *The Good Companions* particularly well.

SAM
Yes, I remember them, too. It's a charming volume, isn't it?

155

ALICE

Oh, but it's more than charming. I think it's profound.

SAM

Do you, do you . . . Well, you may be absolutely right. . . . It is, of course, not by me but by Mr. Priestley, but that doesn't matter. The important thing is that it was written, don't you agree?

ALICE

Oh dear! You must forgive me. (*Suddenly very loud*) I do such a lot of reading.

SAM
(*Resolved to shout back*)
And I do comparatively little writing! Now, that's enough about me.

TOMMY

Alice knows more about your works than I do.

SAM

Is that a source of pride in you, Tommy?

TOMMY

What?

SAM

Your ignorance of my work?

TOMMY

Well, I'm just not a literary type, am I?

156

SAM

No, and then of course I know very little about immigration.
Now, Montego —

ALICE

Oh, Alice, please! It's a revolting name, isn't it? Except that
the others are worse. Aspasia, Lettice, Oona, O'Shaughnessey,
Delagrange, Clavering.

SAM

Congratulations.

ALICE

What on?

SAM

Your memory.

ALICE
(*Laughing*)
It is a bit of a mouthful, isn't it?

SAM

Now tell me, Clavering, what are your interests, my dear! You
look like . . . an artist of some sort.

ALICE

Oh, I don't know, I did dabble in sculpture for a while.

TOMMY

Yes, damned interesting stuff.

157

SAM

Really.

ALICE

I gave it up, though. It's quite interesting, but it's filthy, isn't it, sculpture? All that clay all over the place.

SAM

You might try wood or stone.

ALICE

I'm an awful coward, I'm afraid. I'm terrified of cutting my fingers.

SAM

There's no point in living in fear. You're right to give it up.

ALICE

Then what else? I did a cookery thing for about six . . . no, five months . . . it was part of a domestic science course, but I didn't take the rest.

SAM
(*After a moment*)

A checkered career!
(ALICE *looks at* TOMMY)

TOMMY

It's all right, darling. The old man's a tease.

SAM

Have I said anything wrong?

158

TOMMY

Alice is a wonderful rider. She's got her own horses.

SAM

Really.

TOMMY

She was in the running to be an Olympic show jumper.

SAM

I was once in the running to be an Olympic marathon runner
. . . but unlike you, I never had sufficient faith in the animal
world to put my trust in any legs but my own . . .

ALICE

Oh, well, horses are almost human, once you get to know them.

SAM

I'm afraid I've never had the privilege of knowing a horse as
well as that. But I do recognize the truth of your statement the
other way round . . . I have known quite a few humans that
are almost horses . . . especially among the upper classes. Oh,
I must make a note of that!
    (*Delighted with his remark, he makes a quick note of it*)

TOMMY
(*Confidentially*)
Alice's father is *Lord* Montego.

SAM

Oh . . . (*On a sudden and mischievous impulse, Sam pushes*

159

the copy of Who's Who *over towards his son, who handles it like a hot brick, embarrassed and irritated*) I put my hoof in it, didn't I? Now I'm going to redeem myself, Alice, by my considerable knowledge. Montego . . . now that's a Jamaican name, isn't it?

ALICE

Well, no . . . actually it's Spanish. Originally it was pronounced Mon-tee-ho. Some ancestor of Daddy's was washed up in Ireland at the time of the Armada. It's an Irish peerage. But we're all as English as we can be now.

SAM

Yes. Yes, I can hear that!
                    (STELLA *enters in a dressing gown*)

STELLA

What's going on in here? A party?

TOMMY

Hello, Mummy.
                    (*He kisses her warmly*)

STELLA

Tommy! (*Kisses* ALICE) Alice!

SAM

You know Mon-tee-ho, Stella?

STELLA

Of course I do. (*To* TOMMY) Why didn't you come and see me first? It wasn't kind.

TOMMY

I saw a light under Daddy's door. I thought it was about time we let the old boy into the secret.

SAM

Secret? What secret?

STELLA

These two young people are getting married tomorrow. It's a pity your health won't allow you to come to the church.

SAM
(*Pause*)
How long's this been going on?

TOMMY

We've been engaged about six months.

SAM

Six months!

STELLA

We'd have told you before, but we didn't want to risk it, did we Tommy?

161

TOMMY

No, and judging by his first reaction, I think we were quite right. When I asked him whether he had any objection he replied "None at all. What is she? Colored?"

STELLA
(*With an exhalation of disgust*)
That's all he cares.

SAM
(*Protesting*)
It was only my tactless way of saying —

STELLA
Yes, yes, I know. It's always your tactless way of saying . . .

SAM
Well, what the hell do I care what color people are, you silly old woman! What a frightful troublemaker you are!

STELLA
Let's go upstairs to my room. I'll make some tea.

ALICE
Are you sure we're not keeping you up? After all, it's very late.

STELLA
(*All smiles*)
Not at all. Come on.
(*Taking them to the door*)

162

ALICE

Goodbye, Mr. Kinsale.

TOMMY

'Night, Dad.

(ALICE *and* TOMMY *go*)

SAM
(*To* STELLA)
Tommy! Have your tea down here?

STELLA

You need your rest. You're not well. Have you taken your aspirin? No, of course not. I don't even have to look.

SAM

Don't you think I should have been consulted?

STELLA

What for? Tommy's thirty-nine. He can marry whom he wishes. He's just come here out of a sense of family feeling, which is remarkable when you come to think of it. I mean, the family's a joke, isn't it?

SAM

Wouldn't it be a common courtesy for me to be presented to the young lady's father?

STELLA

Her father is Lord Montego.

163

SAM

What about it?

STELLA

He doesn't like your books. He doesn't want to meet you.

SAM
(*Outraged*)

Has he read them?

STELLA

I don't think so. Lady Montego passed away last year.

SAM
(*Sarcastic*)

I'm frightfully cut up to hear about that.

STELLA

You don't care.

SAM

Please have your tea in here, my dear.

STELLA

Why?

SAM

I'm lonely.

STELLA

You're sick.

164

SAM

I would like some company!
(*Inadvertently he puts his cigar into his mouth, then withdraws it, but he is too late*)

STELLA

You're working. We don't want to disturb you. You're smoking!

SAM

What of it?

STELLA

A cigar!

SAM

I suppose you want half of it.

STELLA

Well, if you want to kill yourself that's your business. You're getting absolutely senile, Sam — senile!

SAM

(*Wheeling himself into the center of the room, furious*)
I heard that, Stella! I heard that and I shan't forget it! I've got a memory like a — what's that damned animal — ? Stella! (*No reply*) Oh, I think that's wretched.
(*He is alone. The figure of his father emerges from the shadows*)

REGINALD

You called for company. Here I am.

165

SAM
(*Abstracted*)

Oh, hello, Dad.

REGINALD

Well, did your interview with Tommy go any better than my interview with you?

SAM

No. If anything it was worse.

REGINALD

It only seems worse to you, Sam. You were trying too hard not to repeat my mistakes with you, just as I was trying too hard not to repeat my father's mistakes with me. It's the same story, endlessly.

SAM

I suppose it must be. How depressing!

REGINALD

Cheer up. There are consolations.

SAM
(*Glum*)

What consolations?

REGINALD

Well, it wasn't a bad cigar, was it?
(ELDERLY *enters from the shadows*)

166

ELDERLY

I heard you call for company.

SAM
(*Peering into the gloom*)
Who's that? (*Recognizes* ELDERLY) Oh, it's you. All dressed up and alone? That's unlike you.

ELDERLY

She was always late, if you remember.

SAM

Who?

ELDERLY

I brought a friend to see you.
(CLARICE *enters from the shadows*)

SAM

Clarice!

ELDERLY

She was a phase in our life. A stupid phase, but one which passed the time of day.

SAM

And night.

ELDERLY
(*Smiling*)

And night.

(*They laugh*)

167

SAM

Oh, I'm sorry, Clarice. That was rude. Funny! She looks like Ada Cooney in this light.

REGINALD

By George, it is Miss Cooney. Ada!
(CLARICE *waves coyly*)

SAM

No, it's Clarice. The prostitute with the heart of gold; the most conventional figure in all of literature.

ELDERLY

That doesn't mean she doesn't exist.

SAM

Why did you kill yourself, Clarice?

REGINALD

You killed yourself, Ada? Why?

CLARICE

I got married, and I was neglected. I didn't feel I was of any use to anybody.

REGINALD: ⎱ It was nothing to do with me, then?
SAM: ⎰ You don't blame me for it?

CLARICE

Oh, Lord, no. Before I felt I was useful. I thought I brought a little happiness to . . .

168

SAM

To many people.

CLARICE

Yes.

SAM

Yes. How nice . . .

CLARICE

Oh, I never really thanked you for my necklace.

SAM: ⎱ Oh, think nothing of it.
REGINALD: ⎰ Please, don't mention it.

SAM
(*Turning slowly to* REGINALD)
What, you too?

REGINALD

Turquoise, amethysts and aquamarines. It cost me all of two
hundred pounds.

ELDERLY
(*To* SAM, *who protests, and prepares himself to be cuffed
over the head*)
Shall I tell him? White gold, pearls and diamonds. Ours cost
us seven thousand pounds.

169

REGINALD
(*Laughing*)
Spendthrifts! Good heavens, there's absolutely no need to throw money around like that!

SAM
(*Relieved*)
He's laughing!
(MIDDLE-AGED *appears, with* STELLA MIDDLE-AGED)

SAM
(*Seeing them*)
What are you doing down here?

MIDDLE-AGED
You called for company.

STELLA MIDDLE-AGED
You even called for me by name.

SAM
When?

STELLA MIDDLE-AGED
Just now . . . when I left the room with Tommy and Alice.

SAM
Oh, no, my dear, I wasn't calling you, I was calling that hideous —
(*He indicates the ceiling, bitterly*)

170

STELLA MIDDLE-AGED

I know. But I wanted you to see me at my best, at my happiest. (*To* MIDDLE-AGED) We're just off to Tommy's christening. We're going to make a big effort from now on — for his sake. Aren't we, Sam?

MIDDLE-AGED

We are indeed, my love.

SAM

(*Imitating* MIDDLE-AGED *savagely*)

We are indeed, my love. You look as though you rented that smile together with your morning suit . . .

STELLA

Please don't be unpleasant, Sam . . . today of all days!

SAM

I'm sorry . . . but don't you two children realize you haven't a chance if you make your effort to be pleasant to one another only for Tommy's sake? It's got to be for your own!

MIDDLE-AGED

(*Hotly*)

No, we don't realize that, and we don't want to realize it. You're too old to have much hope. At least, leave us ours.

STELLA

Don't be cruel, Sam! How do I look?

171

MIDDLE-AGED

Not bad . . . all right.

SAM

Oh . . . how pretty you were!

STELLA
(*Turning to* SAM)
Oh Sam . . . thank you for noticing — at last.
(YOUNG *staggers in, wearing running togs*)

YOUNG

I heard you call for company. I came as soon as the race was over.

SAM

Race? What race?

YOUNG

I've just won the Inter-varsity Marathon. I put all I had into that finish, thanks to Stella. If it hadn't been for her, I don't think I could have done it.

SAM

Stella? Was she there?

YOUNG

She was there with Lady Chough. There's talk of me for the first Olympic Games in Athens!

172

SAM

I know. Do keep warm!

YOUNG

Finish your book!

SAM

What do you mean?

YOUNG

There's not much time left.

SAM

What?

YOUNG

It's almost time for the final sprint. I'll lend you all my strength.

MIDDLE-AGED

You've got my integrity.

ELDERLY

You've got my common touch.
(AGNES KINSALE *enters, holding a baby*)

REGINALD

Ah, Agnes. Isn't it past his bedtime?

AGNES

Yes, it is, but I stole him from Nanny for just a moment. He's so new, I still can't get used to him. Isn't he adorable?
(*All except Sam crowd round*)

173

STELLA MIDDLE-AGED

Can he see?

AGNES

The doctors say he can't, or at least, that he sees everything upside down, but I don't believe them. Look . . . his eyes are open.

STELLA MIDDLE-AGED

Oh, he's smiling!

REGINALD

That's gas.

AGNES

Don't you believe it. He's got a sense of humor like his mother.

ADA

What's his name?

AGNES

Samuel.

SAM
(*Feebly to* REGINALD)
Daddy . . . who is that?

REGINALD

That's you. Come and have a look. You called for company.
(REGINALD *pushes the amazed* SAM *in the wheelchair towards* AGNES)

174

SAM

Might I hold it, do you think?

AGNES

If you're very gentle.

SAM

Oh, yes, I'll be very gentle . . .

AGNES
(*Handing him the baby*)
Easy does it. Smile at the old gentleman. There. He likes you.

REGINALD
(*Looking down at the baby*)
He looks so innocent, so helpless, doesn't he?

SAM

Yes . . . yes . . .

REGINALD
(*Slowly and deliberately*)
And yet it's all built in, the prejudice, the fear, the longing,
the desire, the seed . . .
(SAM *lets out a piercing shout of despair*)

SAM

No!

(*The baby begins to cry, fitfully*)

175

AGNES

Oh, what did you do that for? (*Taking the baby*) Come to mother. There, there. You silly old man. I'll take you back to Nanny.

(*She goes off into the shadows, followed by* STELLA *and* ADA. ELDERLY, MIDDLE-AGED *and* YOUNG *move in to* SAM'S *wheelchair*)

YOUNG

That was when the starter had just fired the gun . . . the race is almost over now . . . it's up to you . . .

SAM
(*Very faint*)

I can't.

MIDDLE-AGED

You must!

SAM

I haven't the strength.

ELDERLY

Go on . . . it's the end of the race that counts . . . you can't let us down now.

SAM

What do you want me to do?

YOUNG

Write down what you have to . . . honestly . . . your mis-

176

takes, your stupidities, your shortcomings . . . if you do that your virtues will speak for themselves, and we won't have lived in vain.

SAM

I'm so . . . alone . . .

YOUNG

We'll be with you to the end and we'll cross the line together.

SAM
(*His face lighting up*)
What, all of us? Even him? (*He points at* ELDERLY *with evident delight*) Where's the other one? (*He sees* MIDDLE-AGED *near him, and is satisfied*) In one glorious photo finish . . . All right, I'll try!
(*The three men laugh and go off into the shadows with words of encouragement.* SAM *wheels himself back to his desk. After a moment his delight at the consolation rendered by his other selves evaporates, and he senses his ultimate solitude. Nostalgically he runs his hand over the drawer, and rattles the handle. It is still locked. Suddenly he brightens up*)
Elephant! That's the word!
(*He takes his key and opens the drawer after a guilty look round the room. He seems to remember all his follies and his pleasures. Then his eye catches something lingering in the depths of the drawer. Amazed, he withdraws the empty photo frame, and clutches it to him*)
Oh, Miriam . . . Miriam . . .

177

REGINALD
(*Firm*)

Throw it away.

REGINALD

I had my Miriam, too. She is illusion. She's escape. You're alone, Sam. Face up to it.

SAM

No!

REGINALD

Don't you believe me, even now?

SAM

(*Who is not as moved as he wishes he were*)
Honestly? I don't know. I don't know.

REGINALD

Don't be afraid of doubt. It's not love that makes the world go round, but doubt. It's the price of freedom. With doubt against you, life's confusion — with doubt on your side, it's adventure. Don't be afraid of it. Be a man, before it's too late.

SAM

(*Stung by this, looks at his father resentfully, then back at the empty photo frame. He suddenly sees the ridiculous side of his sentimental outburst, and throws the frame carelessly across the room. After a hesitation, he pulls the drawer out, and lets it fall to the floor with a clatter. He*

178

notes the satisfaction on REGGIE'S *face, takes up his pen, and quickly loses himself in reflection*)

There. I'll leave you now. You're in good hands. Your own.

(REGINALD *turns and walks slowly away into the shadows.* SAM *resumes his writing, deriving evident satisfaction from the sudden tumult of his thoughts, as*

THE CURTAIN SLOWLY FALLS

179